THE FIRST YEAR IS SURVIVAL

The Essential Guide For Parenting Twins & Multiples

LEONIE HUIE

Published in Great Britain by Hashtag Press 2020

Text © Leonie Huie 2020
Cover Design © Helen Braid 2020

A CIP catalogue for this book is available from the British Library.

ISBN 978-1-9162864-3-6

Typeset in Garamond Classic 11.25/14 by Blaze Typesetting

Printed and bound in Great Britain by Clays Ltd, Elcograf S.p.A.

Hashtag PRESS

HASHTAG PRESS BOOKS
Hashtag Press Ltd
Kent, England, United Kingdom
Email: info@hashtagpress.co.uk
Website: www.hashtagpress.co.uk
Twitter: @hashtag_press

I dedicate this book to my mother, June Martin.
Words cannot describe how much I appreciate her, especially
through such a challenging pregnancy and overwhelming
first year as a mother of twins. I don't know what I would
have done without this amazing human being.
I love you Mum.
Don't ever change.

Acknowledgements

This book was written to help support mothers, fathers, carers and family members who have a part in raising multiples. I would like to include a special thanks to all the amazing parents who provided me with their real-life insights into being a parent of twins, triplets or quadruplets. Speaking with you and hearing your experiences made me realise I was not alone with my feelings of anxiousness, tiredness and moments of loneliness during the first year as a mother of twins. Your contributions, advice and tips will help so many other parents about to embark on a journey of multiples and survive the first year.

A sincere thank you to my husband, Josh, for being such a wonderful dad to our twins, who worship him dearly, true Daddy's girls. Thank you for giving me the time to complete this book by keeping our twins occupied and for the contributions you have made to this book, which I'm sure will benefit many new fathers of multiples.

I would like to thank my publishers, Hashtag Press, for making my idea into a reality. Their guidance and support made a challenging journey much easier.

I feel endless gratitude for my mother who raised three daughters on her own - she is a true superwoman. She has taught me how to be fearless, hardworking and resourceful. She is a mum who has made endless sacrifices in her life to raise me and my sisters and always put us first no matter what. An amazing grandmother to her three grandchildren. Thank you for everything mum from the bottom of my heart.

Julia and Monique, my beautiful two sisters. I sincerely thank you both for everything, always there for me, you both know how full on life has be for me with your nieces but there to offer me a helping hand.

To my dad, thank you for just listening at the other end of the phone whenever I needed to speak to you, moments I'll cherish and never forget. Amazing grandparents, my in-laws, always ready to offer a helping hand with the twins whenever needed, the appreciation is endless.

My four-year-old niece Lotus (my little chicken I call her) born at 27 weeks, a survivor, fighter, miracle baby. You have taught me the true meaning of courage, determination and appreciation of the smaller things in life.

The appreciation and love I have for Aunty Emma who helped raise my twins, looked after them whilst my husband and I worked. Taught them how to count, their ABCs and table manners. I am truly grateful for all you have done. And my wonderful cousin Ray-J for being there who the twins love dearly.

I'm a true believer in the saying 'An angel has been sent from above.' My friend Cassandra is that angel. I cannot thank her enough for her love, care and support she has shown me and my twins. Also, always there whenever I need her.

I am forever grateful to my best friends Jazzy and Ayo for their support during my pregnancy and beyond. Having people like these two around you, who you can rely on, talk to at any time and who help you whenever you need them; I am blessed to have such amazing beings in my life who make it so easy not to be afraid to ask for help as a new parent of multiples.

Lastly, I want to thank my twin daughters La Belle and Lourdes who inspired me to write this book to help other parents of multiples survive that all important first year. You are both my heart and soul, and my life has even more purpose now you are both in it. I love you both more than life itself and can't wait for the endless adventures we'll have together as you grow

Table of contents

Introduction

Useful Websites

"Where there is a woman, there is magic."

-Ntozake Shange-

Introduction

Hi, my name is Leonie. Firstly, I want to thank you for reading The First Year is Survival. Whether you are a parent of one child, twins or multiples, I hope you find this book useful. I just want to be clear before you read further; I have based this book on my own experiences as a mother of twins with a little input from my husband from a father's perspective. I have also interviewed mums and dads from around the world to get their views on being parents of multiples and the struggles they have faced. I've included survival tips at the end of each chapter; they come from wonderful parents from around the globe sharing their wisdom and knowledge, which they used to survive the first year of parenthood.

The reason I decided to structure my book like this is because it's not just about what my husband and I went through in the first year of being a parent of twins, or how we survived, it's about what we've all experienced as mothers and fathers raising multiples. We have so much in common but at times it can feel like those early days of parenting are so lonely and isolating. It can feel, when you're in the midst of a sleepless night, that you're the only person awake rocking your baby back to sleep at 3am. And for those parents who have one child at a time, parents planning for a baby or currently expecting, I'm sure you'll be able to read this book and relate to many parts of it.

This self-help guide can be used as an informative tool to help prepare you for the first year of parenting. It is not intended to scare you, or make you worry, but to provide you with some insightful information, increasing your awareness of things that might happen and how best to deal with situations as they arise. As we know, all children are different, and all families are different, but I hope in this book there will be a lot of useful advice to make parenting in your first year that little bit easier.

To give you some more information about me, I'm a mum of fraternal twin girls who I call my twin heartbeats. I'm 39, married to Josh (who I'll talk about in this book), a teacher, entrepreneur, empowerment coach and public speaker. I live in the wonderful, vibrant city of London and haven't slept properly since being five months pregnant! I come from a large family with plenty of twins going back generations. My grandmother, born and raised in Dominica, was one of 14 children and a twin; she had five children including twin boys (my uncles). One of my uncles then had twin boys and I had twin girls. I also have a lot of twin cousins, so twinning is most definitely a thing in my family.

I named my twins La Belle, meaning 'the beautiful' in French (born first, weighing 5lbs) and Lourdes, named after the Roman Catholic shrine Our Lady of Lourdes in Southern France (born second, weighing 4lb 12oz). They were born a minute or so apart by C-section and from that day my life changed forever. I remember being excited and scared at the same time about delivering twins the conventional way, but at 37 weeks and four days my waters hadn't broken, and La Belle was slightly breached. Her head was right under my ribcage, while Lourdes was facing down in the right position. My stomach was very heavy and I was on crutches due to my right hip moving out of place from baby weight.

Our twins were delivered on the morning of Friday 3rd

November 2017 in a hospital room full of consultants, doctors, nurses, midwives and even junior doctors in training, who had asked if they could be in the delivery room. Why not, I'd thought; the more the merrier, right?

I was so excited at finally being able to give birth as I couldn't wait to see my toes again and wear a decent pair of shoes (I had been wearing my husband's flip flops for months as they were the only footwear I could fit into). Whilst in the delivery room, the doctors and nurses had made me feel as comfortable as possible. They were very accommodating. I had my husband and my mother with me in the delivery room awaiting our new arrivals. I was given the option of playing some background music throughout my labour to help me relax, which was nice because I didn't know that was allowed before I went in to give birth. Whenever I tell people what music I was playing they laugh, as they never would have expected to hear me say Hip-Hop.

During my pregnancy I did a lot of research into the different kinds of music to listen to that would help babies to relax, as they were an active pair beyond belief when they were in the womb. They kicked a lot, which was rather uncomfortable at times. I read that developing babies usually start to hear sounds during the second trimester. Classical music was the recommended genre to listen to whilst pregnant, such as piano sonatas by Mozart. I tried it for a while, but it didn't work. It's not the type of music I would normally listen to, so I tried something different.

I like Hip-Hop, soulful house and Jazz music with a little bit of urban. I tried these different types of music with the twins but only one seemed to relax them and stop them from kicking: Hip-Hop! When I played Nas or Jay-Z the twins would stop kicking. I thought this was quite interesting so to test this out properly I played piano sonatas (lots of kicking and discomfort), then played Nas (no kicking), Mozart (lots of kicking and discomfort), then Jay-Z (no kicking).

There you have it, I thought to myself, Hip-Hop it is! So, in the delivery room I played Nas's album, which the girls were born into the world listening to, and it still helps them relax now. Thank you Lord.

I don't know about you but when I was told I was having twins and they could be the same sex or one of each, I'd already made up in my mind what I wanted and what they would look like. As you may already know with fraternal twins, they can look the same, or quite similar, or nothing alike at all. Obviously, I had no say in the sex or appearance of my twins, but it was a nice thought while it lasted. My girls look very different in appearance: one is darker than the other, taller and bigger. They have different personalities: one is needy and clingy and the other is fiercely independent. Aren't genetics amazing?

I decided to write this book due to my traumatising experience when pregnant and during the first year as a mum of multiples. It was an experience I'll never forget. There was so much I wasn't prepared for and I believe future parents can benefit from knowing in advance, especially during the first year of parenting multiples, and I hope that will help make life easier and less stressful

From the day I found out I was pregnant up until the day I gave birth I was in pain. To start with I had an awful tugging pain in my lower abdomen which just wouldn't go away. I remember asking friends when I would start to feel better and be able to enjoy my pregnancy but that never happened. Things just got worse.

I also decided to write this book as I kept a digital dairy of my twins' development. I did this because I wanted something special to give them when they were older. It was quite challenging remembering everything especially because I was doing it twice over. My husband would always say to me, "I don't know where you find the time to do this." But I felt it was important. After all, it's not every day a woman is blessed with having multiples.

When I fell pregnant with twins, I started doing research online about everything there was to know about having multiples (I bet you did this too). I started off with researching how twins are conceived then moved on to the differences between identical and fraternal twins. I found out where twins are most commonly conceived in the world (Nigeria in West Africa). I could go on forever but I'm sure you catch my drift.

I loved looking at twin nurseries, twin clothing, twin prams, twin toiletries etc. I just went a bit twin OTT. I even created different Pinterest boards on twins. I kept thinking to myself that I needed to buy TWO of everything. OMG! Isn't that just a crazy thought? I knew plenty of mothers with just one child who went OTT too, so I jumped right in.

At the end of each chapter I have provided you with a notes section to prepare yourself for what lies ahead, to help you reflect on what you have experienced or to provide yourself with reminders. I have also collated a list of useful websites based on each chapter of this book, which are filled with useful tools, information, advice, help and support throughout your first year as parents. This is the book I wish I'd had during my pregnancy with the twins.

"You look tired."
"That's because I am!"

-Leonie Huie-

CHAPTER ONE

Sleep Deprivation

I decided to start this book with a chapter about sleep deprivation because I felt like it took over my life completely. Never did I understand the importance of sleep until I became a parent. I was fully aware that your sleep pattern changes and you don't get that much sleep, but never in a million years could I have ever imagined the effects sleep deprivation can have on you: physically, mentally and emotionally.

As humans we cannot function sufficiently on a day-to-day basis without the right amount of sleep, but is there actually a right amount? How do we know if we are getting enough sleep? Well, what we do know is that not everyone requires the same number of hours of sleep per night as we all have different lives, jobs and other commitments that play a vital role in how long we sleep for. According to Help Guide (www.helpguide.org), the average adult should get between seven to nine hours' sleep every night to function at their best. I'm sure there are people who function well on six hours of sleep a night, as well as those who don't do so well if they have less than nine hours of sleep per night.

One thing I'm sure we can all agree on are some of the benefits of getting a good night's sleep. It helps to reduce stress levels, makes you feel more energised and helps to put you in a better mood. Some people can get very grumpy when they haven't had a good sleep. The Mental Health Foundation believes that sleep is vital for good mental and physical health, including helping us to recover from mental and physical exertion (www.mentalhealth.org.uk).

Sleep deprivation is not only frustrating and stressful, it can lead to some serious health issues such as heart attacks and strokes, obesity, diabetes, depression and anxiety, and lower fertility rates (www.nhs.uk). This is why it is imperative that we get enough sleep every night to avoid the risk of such health problems occurring in our lives.

However, after giving birth, sleep becomes somewhat of an unspoken word, something we as parents wish for but rarely get. Now, I know a lot of parents are agreeing with me on this because it's something we lack during the first year of parenting, whether we have multiples or just one baby at a time. Either way, the feeling of complete despair is there throughout every part of your being. All we beg for is an hour, half an hour, even five minutes during desperate times! When will it end?

It's quite funny actually because I have met lots of parents who have children in their teens, and they say they *still* lack sleep because of their children... albeit for different reasons! I know if you were to ask my mum, she would be one of them.

"I have three grown daughters who still make me lose sleep. I'm always doing something for one of them."

"But we love and appreciate you mum, so it's okay," I hear myself saying.

I remember reading a newspaper article during my pregnancy about the number of hours' sleep a new parent gets. The article said four and a half hours per night on average.

Wow, I remember thinking, *that's not as bad as I thought it might be. I might actually manage to cope on almost five hours of sleep a night with twins.*

I felt somewhat relieved after reading this because I worried a lot during my pregnancy about how I might not cope as a new mum without getting a decent night's sleep. However, this feeling of relief was short-lived. My twins' sleeping routine was painstakingly draining. The lack of sleep in the first year was unreal! It affected me so badly I started to hallucinate. Yes, hallucinate. Sometimes my vision was blurry. I couldn't see or think straight; it was as though I was dreaming but doing so wide awake. I actually felt like I was being punished.

Why is this happening? I keep thinking to myself. *None of my friends told me about this part of motherhood.*

I'm sure some of you know what I'm talking about here; you may have experienced this too. Sleep deprivation was awful for me. I remember falling asleep whilst feeding the twins or burping them. I felt guilty at times because I couldn't remember if they'd burped or not, so I would stay up even longer until I heard them burp. The last thing I wanted was to have to deal with colic again.

Yes, one of my twins had colic during the first couple of months. My husband and I were already struggling with the lack of sleep endured and then colic struck! I didn't even know what colic was; I hadn't heard of it until I called my mum to tell her that La Belle kept crying. I changed her, fed her, tried to soothe her, but she wouldn't stop crying. My mum said it sounded like she had colic so I called my doctor, and took La Belle to the GP, who confirmed it was indeed colic and provided me with a prescription to get her some medication, which was heaven on earth because it started to work straight away.

I started to notice a pattern with La Belle: she was the twin who always got sick. She was the twin who found it rather difficult to sleep, who cried more, who wouldn't latch on when feeding and refused breast milk. I didn't want to label her the poorly twin, but that's just how things seemed. If I'm honest, on reflection, I paid a bit more attention to her than Lourdes because of this. I just worried about her more. Her sister was much more independent.

As well as battling with sleep deprivation and colic, I also battled with breastfeeding. I didn't breastfeed for long. I found it a real struggle with twins and couldn't get to grips with the feeding process, the position of the twins on their pillows when feeding, the different techniques I was shown by the midwives. All of it was too much at one time. I was experiencing some discomfort from my C-section, which required me to take painkillers. My brain couldn't take all of it on at one time, and to be honest, I didn't discuss this with anyone at the time, not even my husband. I was just too tired to speak.

I also suffered from postnatal depression and anxiety the first few months after childbirth, which I will go on to explain in more detail in Chapters three and six. I thought I was a bad mother because I couldn't breastfeed. I felt like the midwives who visited me at home thought I was a bad mother; they often tried to get me to breastfeed and told me repeatedly about the benefits of breastfeeding. I always cried when they left, with feelings of complete overwhelming guilt and despair. I explained this to my husband at the time, but he didn't understand what I was going through. Honestly, I don't think I even fully understood myself either.

My husband was struggling in his own way with working long hours and coming home to twins and not getting any sleep. I used to sit by the front door and wait for him to come home so I could hand over the twins and get some sleep; that was the plan anyway, but it hardly happened. By the time Josh came home he was exhausted. I could see it in his eyes: he wanted and needed sleep as much as I did. We were both suffering from sleep deprivation beyond extremes.

As much as I struggled with breastfeeding, I really did try to tandem feed (feed at the same time) but La Belle just wouldn't latch on and became very irritable, which then caused Lourdes to become irritable. I'm sure they sensed my anxiety as I was so frustrated and disappointed in myself for not being able to breastfeed my babies. I even tried to feed them one at a time, which worked for Lourdes but not La Belle. In the end I gave up expressing milk and bottle-fed from around six weeks old as they weren't getting enough milk through breastfeeding.

I really wanted to breastfeed, not just because of the benefits to my girls but I thought it would also help me lose weight. By two months, the girls were fully on formula milk. Every time I fed them all I could hear was a little voice in my head echoing what the midwives had said, "Babies get all their nutrition through breast milk." I felt terrible and this horrible feeling went on for the next few months.

Another thing that made the lack of sleep so challenging throughout the first year was the fact that the twins did not always feed and sleep at the same time. People would always comment about doing things at the same time with the twins to make our lives easier—trust me, I would have loved that to happen—but you can't force multiples to feed at the same time, let alone sleep at the same time (not my twins for sure). This meant zero sleep for me. Let me give you an example.

During the period of the twins being two to four months old, when I would put them to sleep, one twin would sleep before the other. When I eventually got the other one to sleep and then tried to get some rest myself, the first twin to fall asleep would wake up. What do you do in a situation like that? It happened all the time.

The best survival tool I used at that time was tears. Yes, I just cried. I would cry out my frustration, cry out my annoyance, cry out my tiredness and yes, relieving myself of all those tears made me feel better. My husband could see I was struggling but did not know how best to help me. We took turns trying to get a nap whenever we could, but they never seemed long enough. An hour's sleep felt like five minutes. Honestly, it was the worst. I just wanted it to be over.

I remember asking my mum, "When will things get better?" I'm sure I asked her this on a daily basis and the response was always the same:

"Soon Lee, soon. The tiredness won't last forever."

I felt like I was stuck in it forever. It was a forever with no sleep: forever tired, forever crying, forever and ever.

When the twins were around six months, we managed to get them into a better routine for feeding and sleeping at the same time. This made a huge difference as we were able to sleep when they did, even just for a few hours.

I remember my sister saying to me, "Try and sleep when the girls sleep."

This worked for a short while until La Belle ended up hospitalised twice for gastro-oesophageal reflux disease (GORD). This occurs when stomach acid frequently flows back into the oesophagus. This backwash (acid reflux) can irritate the lining of the oesophagus. In our daughter's case, her milk was getting stuck in her windpipe and cutting off her air supply. Having to give my six-month-old baby CPR was by far the worst experience of my life. She stopped breathing and turned blue around her mouth and nose. Her body lay lifeless and I thought I'd lost her. When this happened, I had to perform CPR twice and I felt like my life ended both times. I will explain more on this traumatic time in Chapter Three.

My sleeping pattern, which I was slowly easing into, became non-existent. I spent almost two weeks in hospital, and didn't have one night of decent sleep. It was so hard to shut off due to the noise of the hospital machines on the ward, the nurses and doctors checking on La Belle and all the tests she had to have in different parts of the hospital. That's not to mention the other babies on the ward crying and me missing my other daughter. I could not wait until I got home.

One morning, whilst on the ward, two consultants came to check up on La Belle and run some tests. They were asking me questions about her health and explaining the different tests they were going to carry out on her that day. One of the consultants asked me how I was feeling. I explained I hadn't slept properly since arriving and then burst into tears. I don't know where the tears came from but in that moment I felt extremely overwhelmed and realised it was the first time I'd cried since performing CPR on my daughter. I think the shock of having to do that blocked my tears.

I kept thinking that I'd be able to sleep better in my own bed once we returned home, but when we eventually got home I had this harrowing feeling in the pit of my stomach that if I closed my eyes something bad would happen to La Belle. I can honestly say this feeling made me believe I could never sleep again. I remember watching over La Belle like a hawk when she was awake, even more so when she was asleep, terrified it might happen again. So, I stayed awake, I kept my eyes open, I watched her every move.

My levels of stress and anxiety were beyond belief. I knew I had to do something because the lack of sleep was making me ill. I was moody, irritable and wasn't eating properly, which had a major adverse effect on my physical and mental health, and wellbeing. My sleeping pattern went from four to five hours per night to about two hours. I put on a lot weight, my short-term memory was affected and I suffered from acute insomnia. It felt like I was living a lifetime of physical and emotional pain, like I was dying on the inside. I had no fight left in me. I had no hope that things would get better. I gave up on myself.

When the twins were around nine months old I started therapy. I was referred by my health visitor. I was gradually able to start to sleep a bit better. Who knew talking to a complete stranger about what happened to your child would make you feel human again? After a few sessions I started to feel more like my old self and managed to get back into a routine of sleeping when the girls slept. My husband also managed to sleep, which meant we could both function better on a day-to-day basis.

Here are some of the things we tried with our multiples to improve sleep for the whole household:

- Work on getting your children into a sleeping routine: morning, afternoon and night.
- Try to sleep when they are sleeping.
- Buy a baby monitor so you can hear them if they stir when sleeping or wake up. Some baby monitors have screens so you can also see them when they are asleep.
- If you are breastfeeding, express enough milk so it can be transferred into little pouches and put them in the freezer. You can then defrost them when needed ready for a feed.
- Ask family/friends to come over to watch your children while you sleep.
- If you are struggling to get your children to sleep, ask your doctor or health visitor to recommend a sleep therapist. Also ask family and friends; they might have used one before.
- Take sleeping shifts with your partner so that you both get a good amount of sleep.
- Ask a trusted friend or family members to watch over the babies while you sleep during the day. It may not be ideal but at least you'll get some sleep. If you have that to look forward to it can also help get you through the sleepless nights, knowing you will get some rest later.

Survival tips for sleeping

Paul-Michael from London, UK.
Father of twin girls aged three.
"In order to sleep better in your first year of parenting it is advisable to have your children in a good sleeping routine. This will help you to sleep better and you will know roughly how long you can sleep for, in case you want to sleep when they are napping, which will allow you to wake up a bit earlier before the babies to prepare feeds etc.

My wife and I had incredible help from her mother and sister, which meant if we needed to sleep, we had family around to look after the twins whilst we did so. As the dad, yes, I had more sleep than my wife and this was because she was breastfeeding and had to wake up during the night for feeds. However, to support her in getting some sleep, when the twins woke up around 6:30–7am, I would spend time with them for a couple of hours before I went to work.

If you are a new dad or it's your first set of multiples, my advice to you would be to always ensure you are aware of your children's sleeping routines. Support your partner, help with bedtime if you are home so you get used to your children's pattern. It's also good to read to your children; the sound of your voice can help soothe them and doing skin-to-skin can really help with bonding. Lastly, try not to fear being a dad. I know it can get overwhelming at times, but relish and live for it!"

Debora from London, UK.
Mother of twin boys aged seven.
"Try to feed them at the same time and wrap them in a swaddle

or baby sleeping bag to avoid too much movement during the night. This is cosier for them. I also fed one twin then the other straight away, so they got used to feeding at the same time. Consistency is important. The whole point here is to make feeding and sleeping easier so that you, as parents, don't get too overwhelmed with it all."

Charlotte from London, UK.
Mother of triplets, two boys and one girl aged seven.
"Sleeping for us with triplets was a real challenge so we employed a maternity nurse (also known as a night nurse) to help with them. If you can do this, it is very helpful, especially when you need sleep. Also, if one baby wakes up for feeding, wake them all up to feed at the same time. Routine is really important with children; prepare feeds in advance to save time. Remember breast milk can be frozen. Please ask for help/support if you feel you need it because it can take its toll on you. Lastly, be kind to yourself. You may feel overwhelmed at times so if you can find some time to rest, do so. When the babies sleep, you sleep."

Josh, London, UK.
Father of twin girls aged two.
"If you have a partner then share feeding times. The mother can express milk which the partner can give to the babies—that way both parents can get some sleep. Both parents can do skin-to-skin as it helps the baby to sleep to relax, which means you get to sleep too. Most importantly, if your babies are really unsettled, which my wife and I experienced at different points, seek support from your doctor/midwife/health visitor/

obstetrician about sleeping advice. In addition, ask your family, friends, neighbours, anyone who can help. We also got advice from a sleep therapist who gave some useful tips for our twins such as having set nap times and sleep times to get them in a good routine and to make your home calm and quiet as bedtime approaches."

Kris from California, USA.
Mother of triplets, two boys and one girl aged two.
"Between breast pumping, feedings and fussy babies not sleeping, I was exhausted. I know some people employed a night nurse but even though you aren't guaranteed sleep, you're guaranteed some help, and consider getting someone who can help with housework.

The sleep deprivation for us was unreal with triplets; no one can prepare you for this. We did have family support, which was great and extremely helpful. But sometimes it's hard to tell family members what needs to be done and those things are usually only done during the daytime hours. It was the night times when we needed a lot of help. If you do have family ask them to help with chores such as unloading the dishwasher, taking out the garbage, making meals—menial household tasks are helpful and will take stress off you as a new parent who just wants to sleep!"

Suzanne from London, UK.
Mother of twin boys aged six.
"My advice to new parents is that it's important to prioritise tasks that you must do. Avoid trying to do everything at once. I tried to do this and it left me feeling burnt out. For example,

when the twins were asleep, instead of getting some sleep at the same time, I would do housework and cooking to try to get it out of the way. So, my advice would be to sleep when the babies sleep and don't do any housework—it can wait. It is more important that you rest so you have enough energy for when the babies wake up.

I survived this with the help and support I received from my husband. Even though he was at work during the day, when he came home, he helped a lot with the twins. I would also say it is important to maintain a good level of communication with your partner so you can better manage your household. I also had two older sons aged 10 and 13 at the time, who were supportive. They were at an age when they were independent and could help with basic tasks around the house.

After a few months of telling myself I couldn't do this anymore and I needed to find time to sleep, I changed my priorities. I stopped the cleaning, tidying up, washing clothes, cooking and made sure I slept. I needed it and it made me feel better.

It's important that you eat well. Having a healthy balanced diet whilst caring for newborns is vital. Eating the right foods keeps your energy levels high. I also did some light exercise by getting some fresh air through taking short walks, and this aided in me sleeping better through the night. In addition to this, try to take time out for yourself—self-care is especially important."

The comments from other parents of multiples just goes to show that we all have our struggles as new parents regardless of how many children we have. We all try different ways to make our children as comfortable as possible, as well as making our lives easier as parents, so that we can get a good night's sleep to do the same thing all over again the next day.

I can really resonate with these tips as all children aren't the same, so we try a range of ways to suit our children's needs to make them comfortable. Like Suzanne said, it's really important to find time for some self-care and have a good, balanced diet to keep our energy levels up.

I believe it's highly important that you find some sort of routine to help your babies sleep at night so that you can do the same. It may be tough to start with but perseverance is key. Doing things such as changing your room layout or moving the position of your babies' Moses baskets or cots can help them sleep better, which means you sleep better. Doing skin-to-skin is both beneficial for them and you, as skin-to-skin can help build attachments and a bond between babies and parents.

I remember my midwife advising my husband that he should do skin-to-skin so the babies could bond with him too. He really enjoyed these moments, saying this helped him to relax. It was one of his favourite ways to rest with the girls. He would remove his vest and lay with them on his chest, so they had skin-to-skin contact for hours.

I have provided some space on the next page for you and your partner to complete as a reminder of the importance self-care. You can list the different things you can do to help you sleep better and take better care of your health and wellbeing, which also helps you get a better night's sleep. Once you have listed your ideas, drawing upon tips you've read in this section and those you've been told by well-meaning friends and family, it will be your own personal tool to use whenever you feel like you need more sleep, and a reminder of what you can do to take better care of yourself. For example, you might add the following to your list:

- Improve diet by eating three meals a day including five to seven fruits and vegetables.
- Take multivitamins to increase energy levels.
- Sleep when children sleep.
- Go for short walks.
- Take it in turns to share nap times with your partner.
- Ask friends/family to look after the babies once or twice a week during the afternoon naptime so you can look forward to some decent sleep for a couple of hours.

My Notes

Steps we're taking to help with sleep deprivation

What works? What doesn't? What do you want to try next? Make your notes here and keep a track of what is actually working!

"Have nothing in your house that you do not know to be useful or believe to be beautiful."

-William Morris-

CHAPTER TWO
Being Organised

Being organised is all about making choices and ensuring the different tasks you need to do are effectively completed. It also helps to make life a little less arduous when things are structured and in order.

Managing that work/life balance can be somewhat challenging when you have so many things to do at work as well as at home. That's why being organised is so important and yes, there are health benefits too, such as reducing stress levels.

High stress levels can lead to health-related problems such as heart disease and depression. Being organised can help increase energy levels, productivity and better eating habits. You'll have more energy to cook healthy meals instead of buying takeaway meals. Most importantly (I think), being organised can make you happier because you will feel more in control. Now, that's something I think we all need a little more of.

Being organised before your children are born is helpful because when they do eventually arrive you can enjoy the time you spend with them instead of worrying about what you need to buy, where to move your furniture, how to put the cot together, or what colour to paint the nursery etc.

I was one of those mums who, once I found out I was pregnant, went into organisation mode, and started to think about all the different things I needed to do before my due date. There was so much going on in my head at one time I'm surprised it didn't explode into images of twin baby outfits! I spent so much time on Pinterest looking at different outfits for twin girls—so cute might I add.

In this chapter I'll talk about my organisational journey whilst being pregnant and in the first year of parenthood. What a whirlwind it was for me going from Mrs Organised to Mrs I Don't Give a Damn in the space of four weeks after the twins were born.

On a scale of one to ten, how organised are you?

I would rate myself a 10 because I am a very organised person in both my home and work life, which were running smoothly in the direction I wanted them to go. I think being a teacher contributed widely to my organisational skills. However, this 10 plummeted to a big fat zero after giving birth.

Organised, what's that? What does it even mean with newborns? Well, for me, my organisation turned into anxiety and postnatal depression. My friends with children would tell me how important being organised with a newborn was, so my husband and I collated a list of items to purchase for our girls whilst I was two months pregnant. We were proud of ourselves because we managed to purchase most of the items on our list by the time I was six months in. Yes, we had a long list, and the reason for it being so long was that our list was in sections to ensure we covered everything we needed to do:

- Section one – Items to purchase for twins including clothing.
- Section two – Reorganising home/moving furniture.
- Section three – Decorating home.

I highly recommend that every pregnant couple has an extensive list. Of course, I would say that, as I'm a fan of being organised. It's all about doing what is going to help you feel more in control, calmer and happier in the long run though. I find that with a list it's so much easier to tick things off as you go. You may realise there are some things on the list you no longer need, but the point is that you write everything down to help organise yourselves more efficiently.

I found out I was pregnant at four weeks so we had plenty of time to plan and prepare for our twins' arrival. I remember complaining to my husband about stomach pains. I thought my endometriosis had returned, a condition I have had since I was 21 years old. It's when parts of the tissue that lines the uterus (endometrium) grow on other pelvic organs, such as the ovaries or fallopian tubes, and cause pain in your pelvis area. Endometriosis can affect women of any age. It's a long-term condition that can have a significant impact on your life especially if untreated. So, I called 111, the NHS advice line, as my pain wasn't severe enough to call 999.

I explained to the paramedic about the pain I was having. She advised I go to my nearest hospital's gynaecology and early pregnancy walk-in service.

I remember saying, "I don't need to go there. I'm not pregnant."

She explained to me that it's not a department just for

pregnancy; they also check other issues for women including providing blood tests and scans. So that morning I went to the hospital. I had to provide a urine sample and then waited to see the doctor. Whilst waiting I asked one of the nurses if she could give me my pregnancy test results because all I was thinking was once pregnancy was ruled out maybe they could give me a blood test or scan to see if the endometriosis had returned. To my surprise the nurse told me that I was in fact pregnant and I stared at the wall in front of me thinking, *What on earth I am going to do now?*

I was eventually called in to see the doctor who gave me a transvaginal ultrasound. I remember her speaking to her colleague, who was also in the room and operating the scan machine.

"Oh, I'll be back in one second," she said before she left the room.

She had left me with my legs in the air with no explanation as to where she had gone!

When the doctor came back she said to me with a big smile on her face, "Wow, would you like the first lot of good news or the second lot of good news?"

I looked at her dumbfounded. I had no idea what she was talking about.

She then said, "You're having twins! Congratulations!"

"What?" I replied. I was completely stunned.

I was told I was pregnant, then I was having twins, all in the space of 10 minutes! My life was about to change forever and I wasn't prepared.

Pregnancy really helped me to put into perspective the short period of time I had to organise myself with everything I needed to do before the babies arrived. I needed to change my mindset as my household was about to double in size. I really wanted everything organised and ready by the time I reached nine months so I could relax for the last two months of my pregnancy. I made sure my current furniture was rearranged accordingly with easy access to items needed when feeding or changing the girls.

Luckily for us we already had self-storage and we had moved around some furniture so we didn't really need to make room for the twins. I had most things planned out and in place until I attended my third maternity physiotherapy appointment during August, week 24 of my pregnancy.

My physiotherapist noticed that I was wobbling left to right when I was walking.

"How long have you been doing this?" she asked me.

"For a few weeks as it helps me to walk better because the weight on my stomach is so heavy. Also it helps with the pain in my back," I explained.

"The way you're walking is rather dangerous and it can cause your hip to become unbalanced, putting even more pressure on your waist. Let me check you over."

She went on to examine me and after a while of having me stretch, move around and balance, she examined my hips. My right hip was out of place from the weight of carrying the twins. My waist was struggling to cope. I didn't think it was an issue, assuming things would be fine once I delivered twins.

'Well that might not be the case," she said, when I expressed my thoughts. "It will be best if you use crutches daily."

Honestly, I thought she was joking when she said that. Only when she handed me the crutches did I take it seriously.

"I'm not using them! It's not necessary."

"I'm afraid you don't have a choice," the physiotherapist said. "Unless you want to cause yourself permanent damage?"

So I left the hospital with two crutches in tow, wondering how I was going to cope! All that was going through my head was:

- I still have things to do before the twins come.
- I still need to decorate.
- I still need to put a few bits in storage.
- I still need to do this, that and everything else!
- How would I rate my organisational skills at that stage? Zero!
- How was I going to organise the little time I had left before the twins' arrival?

I admit it, I went into serious panic mode. I cried and kept telling myself everything was going to be okay. I tried my best to stay optimistic, but I knew it would be challenging.

As I was stuck in panic mode, anxiety decided to join the party. I felt I was no longer in control of my life. I had to rely on others to do things for me. My husband couldn't help much because he was at work so I had to wait until weekends to sort things out for the twins. My to-do list seemed to get longer and longer.

When reflecting on this experience one thing I learnt was that when you are pregnant you can't predict how your pregnancy will go. So it's best to do things sooner rather than later and get those around you to help and support you if you can.

My twins arrived on the 3rd November 2017 and I thankfully had most things organised at home. The sleeping and changing area was what I used most and I had everything I needed, but my list still incomplete in other areas.

With all the different things I had to do with the twins, such as feed them, burp them, bathe them, change them, try to get some sleep if possible, cook, clean, do laundry and iron, how was I supposed to complete my list?

"Lee, forget the list, there are only a few things on it and none of them are urgent," Josh said to me one day.

I told him I would forget it, but I just couldn't let it go. Being the organised person I am it was bugging the hell out of me and then, a few days later, I remember trying to get out of bed but I couldn't; my stitches from my C-section were causing me agonising pain. I couldn't do anything, and I mean anything.

The twins were about four weeks old at the time and I couldn't even pick up them up. I couldn't sit up, I couldn't feed my girls. Nothing! I felt paralysed. I needed to tidy up and wash some baby clothes but I just couldn't move.

I got Josh to call my doctor who I spoke to on the phone and he advised me to call 999 but I didn't want to leave the girls. I called my mum and told her my symptoms and she advised I go to A&E, but I ignored them both. Instead, I took some painkillers and the pain started to ease and in that moment I realised why I was in so much pain. It was my own fault. I had clearly forgotten what the doctor had said to me at the hospital before I was discharged.

After giving birth at the hospital I was advised to rest as much as I could.

"Having a C-section is major surgery, and it takes time to heal, so avoid doing anything strenuous," I remember the doctor telling me. "It can take up to six months for a C-section to heal, therefore, in the meantime, reduce your movements and rest as much as possible."

"Really doctor?" I said, thinking to myself, *How does a mother with newborn twins rest?*

There I was, still trying to be Mrs Organised with newborn twins, operating on no sleep since I'd arrived home. Clearly it wasn't working for me therefore something had to change. So, one day I stopped caring what my house looked like.

I soon forgot about completing my list and instead I made sure that I rested like the doctor said. That was it for me. No more trying to keep things tidy, no washing clothes, no cooking, no cleaning, especially hoovering—all that movement was putting strain on my stomach which needed to heal. My healing actually took a year and not six months like the doctor had said.

I asked for help from my family and friends who really supported me through the first few months of parenthood. My husband hired me a nanny who we had for a couple of months to help look after the girls, iron clothes and do some cleaning, which made a huge a difference. I was finally able to get some sleep.

My advice would be to have a list prepared as early as possible but don't worry too much if you haven't got everything on it; the essentials are the most important things. For example, when our twins came home from the hospital, we had purchased two Moses baskets for them to sleep in. We hadn't got around to buying everything on my list, including a cot, due to me being on crutches and I didn't want to order one online. I wanted to see it at face value.

However, at two to three months we eventually bought a cot which the twins topped and tailed in. There we were, thinking how organised we were with sleeping arrangements, but the cot ended up becoming a disaster. Our twins were very unsettled in it—they wouldn't sleep and they cried a lot whenever they were put in it, so we had to change sleeping arrangements and ended up buying them an adjustable single bed. One of our best buys. Their sleep pattern slightly improved and we became more organised with bedtime routines.

So try to be organised and complete as much as you can on your prepared list, starting with *essential* buys. The rest can come later as you might not even need them.

Survival tips for being organised

Anna from Essex, UK.
Mother of quadruplets, two girls and two boys aged three.
"I can imagine that being organised and preparing for the arrival of one newborn must take some work, but in my case, I had to prepare for four. Having quads involves a lot of organisation and I've learnt what works best and what doesn't as my children have got older.

When I was pregnant, I knew there were a lot things that my husband and I needed to prepare at home ahead of their arrival, but it wasn't something we could focus on due to one of the quads being very small in weight compared to the rest; when she was born we were informed she might not survive. We didn't know if we would be bringing home four or three children, so our focus was on our baby girl in the NICU. I was so overwhelmed with relief when quads came home, then we had to get really organised in a short space of time, which was hard work as we didn't have much support from family or friends. It was just me and my husband with four newborns.

One thing I did, which made life easier and gave me time to do other things in between feeds, was to give quads their milk all at the same. This was challenging I had six bottles per baby and ensured their feeds were always ready. I also put their names on their bottles, so I knew whose feed belonged to who, which really helped.

I would advise you prepare a list of things to buy newborns, try to avoid buying too many baby clothes as babies grow quickly and all these clothes can take up unnecessary space in your home. This also applies to baby equipment. We did not buy four of everything. For example, we purchased three baby rockers instead of four and the two girls didn't even use them as they preferred being comforted on a pregnancy pillow. The boys loved the baby rocker and were able to relax in it. This may be different for twins or triplets, but we realised quite early on that they each had different habits and preferences. Organise your living room so you have essential items to hand and the space you need to move around freely.

Doing these little things helped us, as a family, survive the first year of parenthood much better."

Charlotte from London, UK.
Mother of triplets, two boys and one girl aged seven.
"It's important to establish a routine early on. Try to stick to it if you can because consistency is so important with multiples. Try not to over-buy products. Babies really do grow fast and you won't get to use everything you have."

Alan from Essex, UK.
Father of twin boys aged seven.
"To help you stay organised I would advise buying nappies and wipes in bulk to avoid you having to constantly go to the shops to buy more. Make more storage space for baby clothes and baby products. We found when you are buying for twins, you should double everything, and you need to put it somewhere easily accessible. If possible, try to keep things tidy to help maintain order. Things can get on top of you at times so being organised is important."

Anna from London, UK.
Mother of twin girls aged three.
"Honestly, I wasn't very organised during my pregnancy when it came to purchasing baby items for our daughters. I kind of did everything last minute because I just wanted to make sure the twins were okay before I bought anything. Most items were purchased towards the last few weeks before I gave birth. I had to rush round to get the essential items such as nappies, wipes and a changing table. I would suggest you try to avoid overspending because babies grow so quickly, and they don't always get to use everything they have. Prepare yourself earlier on in your pregnancy. Try not to stress out. You'll most probably get lots of gifts from family and friends so I'm sure you'll end up with all you need."

Ebony from London, UK.
Mother of twin girls aged nine.
"If you need to, it's best to reorganise your furniture before your babies arrive, so you don't have worry about doing any of that whilst you are trying to look after them."

Cassie from London, UK.
Mother of twin boys aged eight.
"I would say I was rather organised with preparing for the twins' arrival; during my pregnancy I made a list of things I needed for them. I attended baby shows to see what was on the market. I also had a list of things to buy from Mothercare, which was useful as I got a lot of things from there. I watched some YouTube videos, which were very useful in helping me organise myself. Our twins were delivered at 36 weeks—a natural

birth—and even though I suffered from back pain it didn't stop us from having a routine with the twins, which was so important. I watched videos on how to organise yourself with babies whilst pregnant. We had set times for bath time, feeding and sleep to help get the twins into a routine."

As you can see from the tips provided by some parents, there are different ways to organise yourself during and after pregnancy. Buying too many baby items can be a waste of money because your babies will grow so fast they may not be able to wear everything they have. As long as you have the essentials, you're fine to start off with.

I honestly had no idea what those essentials were. I had to research this online, because all that was going through my head was, *Whatever I buy, times that by two*. So, here's a little helping hand. Just in case you need an essential guide of what to buy, I have provided you with one on the next pages. Please note this is just a guide based on what I bought. What you buy is at your own discretion and will therefore vary from household to household and may also depend on the number of multiples you have and what time of year your children are born. So, you might buy winter coats if your babies are born in the winter/autumn season or you might buy more vests/tops if your babies are born in the summer season. These are little things to consider before buying clothing items, and it does save money. I hope this helps!

Essentials for newborn multiples

Bedroom/nursery
- Moses basket/crib x2.
- New mattress for each Moses basket/crib and bedding x2.
- Baby monitor x1.
- Night light x1.

Clothing
- All-in-one sleepsuits x2, pack of 8.
- Short-sleeve bodysuits x2, pack of 8.
- Long-sleeve bodysuits x2, pack of 8.
- Soft booties x6 pairs.
- Scratch mittens x6 pairs.
- Socks x8 pairs.
- Newborn bibs x2, pack of 10.
- Hats x6.
- Cardigans x6.
- Jackets/onesies for the pram x4.

Travelling/getting around
- Double buggy (detachable car seats).
- Car seats – if you drive (Group 0, Group+ or Group 0+/1).
- ISOFIX – clip-in/out seat base.
- Blankets x4.
- Baby carrier x2.

A tip for drivers

Keep a box in the boot of the car to store baby items and remember to keep it replenished. I kept a box from when my twins were four months old and it was so helpful. Sometimes I found myself in a rush to be somewhere and would forget something I didn't pack in the twins' baby bag. This box contained the following items and always came in handy, in fact, I still use it now:

- Nappies.
- Nappy bags.
- Wipes.
- Muslins.
- Cream.
- Onesies.
- Vests.
- Tops.
- Trousers/leggings.
- Socks.
- Booties.
- Gloves.
- Hats.
- Coats.
- Blankets.
- Buggy rain cover.
- First aid kit.
- Soft toys and teething rings.

Below are some useful websites to help you with essentials for twins and multiples:

- www.nhs.uk
- www.babycenter.com
- www.twinsmagazine.com
- www.thebump.com
- www.parents.com

How organised are you? Have I given you some food for thought? Do you know what you need to buy for your new arrivals? Are you planning on decorating or rearranging furniture? Have you made a list? Get your partners, family or friends ready to help move or assemble furniture to ensure you have what you need in place before babies arrive.

Please use the following page to make notes on anything you and your partner might need to do; use it as a reminder or to bullet-point those free-flowing ideas you have to help you both put plans into action and better prepare yourself before your multiples arrival.

My Notes

Use this space to plan and prepare

My Notes

Use this space to plan and prepare

"You don't have to see the whole staircase, just take the first step."

-Martin Luther King-

CHAPTER THREE

Anxiety

In this chapter I will be talking about the different types of anxiety, symptoms, risks and treatments available. This is a very significant chapter for me as anxiety has been a big part of my life for many years and for most of those years I had no idea I had it, or what it was. I was even more shocked when I found out it was a mental health disorder.

Here, I will be explaining how I have learnt to cope with the condition and why it's so important you ask for help if you suffer from anxiety. It's a condition I believe needs the right amount of attention in order for it to be treated accordingly, and because there are different types of anxiety there is no single treatment universal for all.

Over the years I have unfortunately seen countless negative perceptions of anxiety; some people are even looked upon as weak because of the condition, which is a shame because having anxiety is far from you being weak. It's a condition with a wide range of treatments that can help you manage it.

Anxiety can affect anyone at any age. There are so many

people who have it but go undiagnosed and don't seek treatment or advice about how to manage the condition. Most people have experienced a feeling of anxiousness at some point in their life which may have involved some or all of the following:

- Having a panic attack.
- Shaking/trembling.
- Tightness of the chest.
- Fast-paced heartbeat.
- Sweating.
- Shortness of breath.
- Breathing faster than normal.
- Nausea.
- Depersonalisation.
- Losing control.
- Fear of dying.

Anxiety can be caused by a variety of factors such as stress, a traumatic experience, drugs and/or alcohol and mental health disorders. It's becoming more and more common. Around six million people in the UK suffer from anxiety (www.anxietyuk. org.uk). It is the most common mental health condition in the USA with 40 million people experiencing it (www.adaa.org).

Anxiety is one of the most common mental health problems that occur during pregnancy in the UK with 13% of women experiencing it at some point. It also affects 15-20% of women in the first year after childbirth (www.nice.org.uk). Some of the factors of this are environmental: stress, job/career, studying, personal relationships and finances.

Anxiety can also be genetically inherited meaning if people in your family have it you are more likely to have it. There are medical factors that can cause anxiety such as the side effects of medication or symptoms of a disease (www. medicalnewstoday.com).

Here are five major types of anxiety that people can experience, including pregnant women. If you had anxiety before pregnancy, experienced it during your pregnancy or are worried about experiencing it when pregnant or after pregnancy, then the information provided below will hopefully be useful to you.

Reading about the five major types of anxiety disorders will help you understand which of these you may have experienced—or are currently experiencing—and how best to address it. If you are concerned about any of these anxiety conditions keep reading to find out additional information and the support available to both mothers and fathers expecting multiples.

The five major types of anxiety disorders are:
1. Generalised Anxiety Disorder (GAD).
2. Social Anxiety Disorder (social phobia).
3. Obsessive Compulsive Disorder (OCD).
4. Panic Disorder.
5. Post-traumatic Stress Disorder (PTSD).

1. Generalised Anxiety Disorder

Generalised Anxiety Disorder (GAD) is when an individual experiences extreme worry about everyday life with no obvious reasons as to why they do so. People with this type of anxiety disorder constantly worry about work, health, finances, family, home life, or school, always expecting some form of major disaster to occur.

GAD can be so severe that it can take over a person's life, as they are continuously worrying or living in fear. It is a feeling of uneasiness about a situation with an uncertain result. The anxiety takes control of their thinking which can hinder functioning on a day-to-day basis, affecting work-life balance such as socialising, work and the relationships they have with people.

Symptoms of Generalised Anxiety Disorder can include:
- Feeling irritable.
- Frequent use of the bathroom.
- Muscle tension/trembling.
- Nausea.
- Headaches.
- Feeling restless.
- Sweating.
- Poor concentrating.
- Extreme worry and tension.
- Tiredness.
- Insomnia.

Risk of Generalised Anxiety Disorder
In most cases, GAD often goes un-diagnosed and may be difficult to differentiate from normal worrying. A woman who was always a worrier may develop GAD during pregnancy, which in some cases can be related to changes with hormone balance, social commitments and mental state. If you have

or think you might have GAD during pregnancy it's very important that you seek medical advice from your GP, midwife or obstetrician, as it could possibly lead to difficulties during pregnancy such as high blood pressure, premature birth, low birth weight and problems with brain development of the baby (www.verywellmind.com).

Treatment for Generalised Anxiety Disorder
Treatment for people with GAD—including expectant mums—will vary according to previous health or medical-related issues and the severity of the anxiety the individual may be experiencing. Treatment is always tailored to the person's needs and will always take into account the unborn babies' health and wellbeing.

Different treatments include:

- Medication: Cipralex, Prozac, benzodiazepines.
- Therapy: Cognitive Behavioural Therapy (CBT).
- Support: family, friends, community groups (face-to-face or online), books, podcasts.

2. Social Anxiety Disorder (Social Phobia)
When researching information into the different types of anxiety disorders, I found that Social Anxiety Disorder (Social Phobia) is the third largest mental health problem in the world, affecting about 7% of the population at any given time. The lifetime prevalence rate (i.e. the chances of developing Social Anxiety Disorder at any time during the lifespan) is about 13% (www.socialphobia.org).

People who have this condition feel intensely uncomfortable

in social situations. It's more than feeling nervous or shy in any given situation; it's a feeling of intense fear of being judged, especially in unfamiliar surroundings or situations where you feel you are being watched or observed by others (www.nhs.uk).

In some cases people with this condition compare themselves to others, afraid they won't measure up, and cannot stop themselves from feeling anxious. Being pregnant with this condition can cause an expectant mother a great deal of stress as she may need to visit her doctor or obstetrician more regularly as well as attending antenatal classes. She may not want to go out as much or be around other people, but at the same time knows the importance of getting checked regularly to ensure the health and wellbeing of her babies.

Symptoms of Social Anxiety Disorder (Social Phobia) can include:
- Low self-confidence/self-esteem.
- Poor relationships with others.
- Shortness of breath.
- Intense worry for days, weeks, or even months before an upcoming social situation.
- Upset stomach, nausea (i.e. butterflies).
- Excessive self-consciousness and anxiety in everyday social situations.
- Extreme fear of being watched or judged by others, especially people you don't know.
- Fear that others will notice that you're nervous.
- Trembling or shaking (including shaky voice).
- Difficulties managing work-life balance.

- Staying quiet in order to escape being noticed or embarrassed.

Risk of Social Anxiety Disorder (Social Phobia)

There are some risks that people with this disorder face which can, in some cases, worsen their condition. Isolating yourself from society may cause you to feel lonely, putting you at risk of suffering from depression. If pregnant or nursing your newborns you should seek help, advice and support from your doctor, midwife or health visitor who are all equipped in helping you receive the best support needed.

Another risk is struggling with new dependants and not asking for help, which can lead to high levels of stress and make anxiety symptoms worse.

Treatment for Social Anxiety Disorder (Social Phobia)

There are two main types of treatment for people (including expectant parents) with social phobias: psychotherapy and medication. In addition to this there is also informal support from family and friends if you feel comfortable enough to talk to them or be in their presence.

- Psychotherapy: counselling or talking therapy
- Medication: Selective Serotonin Reuptake Inhibitors (SSRIs), Paroxetine (Paxil) or Sertraline (Zoloft)
- Support groups: online (Anxiety UK, Mind, Social Anxiety UK).

3. Obsessive Compulsive Disorder (OCD)

This disorder is a common type of anxiety disorder affecting millions of people of all ages all over the world. Commonly known as OCD, this disorder can have a major impact on everyday life for the individual, whether they are a young child, teenager or an adult.

Approximately 2.3% of the global population have OCD, which involves unwanted thoughts occurring, including compulsive, repetitive and uncontrollable behaviours that you feel must be carried out.

Common signs of this disorder can include the constant need to wash your hands, checking that you have locked your front door or that you have turned off the cooker multiple times which affects day-to-day life and mindset. But there is so much more to OCD than this. OCD presents itself in many forms, and goes way beyond the common misconception that it's just a little hand washing or checking light switches here and there.

Doing something over and over again may help a person with OCD feel "better" for a while, but then the anxiety will return and therefore warrants addressing. The World Health Organisation (WHO) states that OCD is one of the top 20 causes of illness-related disability, affecting 1.2% of the population (www.ocduk.org).

OCD affects one in every 100 women in pregnancy. This is similar to the rates in the general population. Some women, during pregnancy or after birth, develop obsessive compulsive disorder, which is called perinatal (prenatal) OCD. This is more common after birth than in pregnancy with about two to three in every 100 women being affected by perinatal OCD in the year after giving birth (www.tommys.org).

Women who have perinatal OCD might have obsessive thoughts about their baby being at risk of harm from an infection or germs, and will spend a long time sterilising or cleaning things over and over again, or if the baby is already born they might constantly check up on them to see if they are breathing. Such compulsive behaviours can cause a mother and their partner a great deal of stress and anxiety during this time.

It's important to recognise the signs and symptoms and be aware of the risks OCD can cause.

Symptoms of OCD can include:
- Constantly washing and cleaning hands.
- Fear of being contaminated by germs or dirt or contaminating others.
- Fear of losing control and harming yourself or others.
- A need for symmetry and orderliness.
- Constantly repeating words in your head.
- Excessive focus on religious or moral ideas.
- Losing things or not having what you might need.
- Asking for constant reassurance.
- Hoarding.

Risk of OCD

There is some evidence that OCD can be genetic and it can occur if you have other mental-health-related issues already and can cause a great deal of stress. OCD tends to start in people during their adolescent years. However, it can affect young children or begin in your 40s. OCD symptoms can get worse during and immediately after pregnancy, perinatal OCD can put a mother and baby at risk such as causing her to have high blood pressure which can affect the baby.

Treatment for OCD
- Therapy: CBT.
- Medication: SSRIs.

4. Panic Disorder

Panic Disorder is when an individual has unexpected and overwhelming feelings of panic or complete fear. It's when feelings of stress, panic and anxiety occur concurrently, which is overwhelming for individuals who have it.

As we know, pregnancy can be a life-changing experience, so feeling worried at this time is perfectly normal. Mums-to-be start to worry about their babies, whether they are eating the right foods, getting enough sleep or sleeping in a safe position to cause no harm to their babies. However, sometimes such anxious thoughts can be a challenge, leading to panic attacks.

During pregnancy approximately 5% of women have panic disorder (www.jamanetwork.com). Panic attacks also affect Dads during their partner's pregnancy because they too worry about their unborn children, their partner's health and wellbeing throughout this time.

If you are pregnant and concerned you might be having a Panic Disorder, there are some symptoms you might experience, which you must inform your doctor about to maintain your (and your babies') health and wellbeing during and after pregnancy.

Symptoms of Panic Disorder can include:
- Racing heartbeat and rapid breathing.
- Excessive sweating.

- Feeling dizzy.
- A numb or tingling feeling in your fingers, toes or lips.
- Tension, pain or trembling in your muscles.

Risk of Panic Disorder
Panic Disorder is nearly two times more common in women than in men. If there is a family history of this disorder you are more likely to get it. High levels of stress can also cause Panic Disorder such as giving birth for the first time, marriage, being a victim of crime, or experiencing a traumatic event in your life.

In addition to this, excessive smoking, drinking, alcohol or drug misuse can all lead to a Panic Disorder. This disorder is very common in those aged 20 to 29 years old but it can start in your teens or when you're 30 or 40 years old.

Panic attacks can impact the foetus, causing a reduced amount of blood to flow to them when the mother has high levels of anxiety. This can cause the baby to have a low birth weight once born and can also cause premature labour (www. nhs.uk).

Treatment for Panic Disorder
- Therapy: CBT.
- Medication: SSRIs, Antidepressants, Pregabalin, Clonazepam.
- Support groups: face-to-face meetings or online (Anxiety UK, social media groups such as closed Facebook pages).

5. Post-Traumatic Stress Disorder
You may have heard of post-traumatic stress disorder, which

is commonly known as PTSD. It's a type of anxiety disorder that can occur in people who have experienced or witnessed a traumatic event in their life such as a serious accident, natural disaster, war or violent personal assault, which leaves a person feeling extremely stressed or frightened.

People with PTSD often suffer from flashbacks or nightmares because of what they experienced which can have an adverse effect on their health and wellbeing, causing some individuals to isolate themselves from society.

PTSD in women can occur before or after pregnancy depending on the type of event that occurred in their life. About one or two in every 100 women have post-traumatic stress after giving birth (www.tommys.org). Some women who have PTSD after pregnancy may have experienced it due to a traumatic childbirth or miscarriage. There is a lot of support available for those experiencing PTSD who are finding it difficult to cope.

Symptoms of PTSD can include:
- Nightmares.
- Flashbacks.
- Emotional numbing: trying to avoid thinking about what happened.
- Sweating.
- Nausea.
- Shaking/trembling.
- Headaches/stomach aches.
- Insomnia.
- Difficulty concentrating.
- Angry outbursts.

• Watching out for danger.

Risk of PTSD

Being at risk of PTSD can lead to depression, other anxiety disorders, substance use-related problems and physical health problems such as diabetes, arthritis, heart, respiratory and digestive-related health issues (www.verywellmind.com). You can be at risk of PTSD if you experienced severe trauma during your childhood, or were raised in an unstable family household or in poverty.

Lastly, if you have a pre-existing emotional or mental health disorder, eating disorder or drug/alcohol abuse attribute you are more likely to suffer from PTSD (www.everydayhealth.com). Thankfully this condition is a treatable one so it is important you seek help if you have any of the symptoms listed above.

Treatments for PTSD

• Psychotherapy: counselling or talking therapy.
• Therapy: Eye Movement Desensitisation and Reprocessing (EDMR), CBT.
• Medication: SSRIs such as Fluoxetine (Prozac), Sertraline (Zoloft), paroxetine (Paxil), Prazosin (Minipress), Clonidine (Catapres), Guanfacine (Tenex), and Propranolol.
• Support groups – face-to-face meetings or online (such as Anxiety UK, MIND, Baby Centre).

Can you imagine experiencing any of these signs or symptoms of anxiety whilst pregnant or as a new parent? Some of you reading this may have already experienced some of these symptoms or are currently experiencing some. It must be extremely overwhelming, especially as it's quite natural for an expectant parent to worry about their unborn children during pregnancy, wanting to make sure their babies are okay.

Parents can experience any of these types of anxiety including dads who might experience signs or symptoms of anxiousness, worry or dread when they are about to embark on a journey of fatherhood of multiples, overwhelmed by concerns about coping with more than one child simultaneously.

I have had two types of these anxieties—GAD and OCD—before and during my pregnancy and still have OCD. My mother believes I've had OCD since the age of two, which honestly doesn't surprise me. She bases this on all the times I spent crying if my hands were dirty, repeatedly tidying up after myself or getting upset if my clothes weren't neat. I was never diagnosed as a child. She said my OCD became more noticeable as I got older.

I didn't notice I had it until I was 18 and living on my own. I then remembered certain events that occurred in my childhood during primary school, which made me realise I've had it for years. I am constantly aware that my twin daughters are at the age where they imitate everything I do.

In this chapter I'll be talking about how anxiety affected me during my first year of parenthood and how I managed to control it with the support of my family, friends and therapist. I will also provide some coping strategies suggested by my therapist to help manage the condition and useful websites for further information and tools to better cope.

I don't know about you but when I found out I was pregnant with twins I felt happy, scared, petrified, excited, confused and anxious all at the same time. You may ask yourself how it's even possible to feel so many emotions simultaneously, but I did and all within the short space of time between being told I was pregnant and finding out I was having twins.

Let me explain.

I suffer from anxiety and have done so for over 30 years. I just wasn't always aware that I had it. I'd never heard of the word as a child; it was never mentioned to me and my doctor never diagnosed me with it. I found out I had GAD when I fell pregnant in 2017. The feelings I had were the same feelings I had experienced as a child in primary school. That awful feeling of dread, being worried all the time, the shaking of the hands and most of all the tightness in my chest.

Even though I realised I had OCD when I was 18, I had no idea it was a type of anxiety disorder until speaking with my therapist. I ask myself every day, all these years later, how have I managed to cope? I never received any medication for it or therapy whilst growing up, I just dealt with it without even having a medical diagnosis until I received therapy a few weeks after finding out I was pregnant.

I was so scared, nervous and worried about my babies that my pregnancy was causing me overwhelming levels of stress, which my doctor was concerned about. He said I could try medication which I didn't want to do, therefore he referred me to counselling. The sessions I attended were really useful and I was provided with different tools to cope whilst pregnant. These sessions took place every two weeks until I was 15 weeks pregnant in June 2017.

I wouldn't go so far as saying my feelings of anxiety had completely disappeared at the end of my therapy, but I did feel more in control. My therapist advised I continue to use the techniques she'd taught me to manage my anxiety episodes when they occurred. I felt quite confident about this as what she suggested had worked in the past. Here were the suggestions she provided:

- Breathing techniques.
- Meditation.
- Counting to 10 slowly.
- Regular exercise.
- Eating a well-balanced diet.

I continued to do this throughout my pregnancy until I was on crutches and encountered problems with my right hip. By the time the twins were born I felt like these suggestions went completely out the window. It was as though the list never even existed. When the twins reached two months old I noticed that my anxiety had returned and each month it got worse, especially by the time they were seven months old—it had got pretty intense.

La Belle had two acute life-threatening events (ALTEs) during the months of May and June 2018, about two weeks apart. As I previously mentioned, she stopped breathing on two separate occasions; she turned blue around her mouth and nose. I will never forget Thursday 24th May 2018 and Saturday 9th June 2018. I had to perform CPR on my baby, giving her mouth-to-mouth resuscitation to revive her, twice. The first time she spent a night in hospital and was monitored by the doctors and nurses.

Words cannot begin to explain my levels of anxiety at this

point in time. All I kept saying to myself was, *Please make my baby be okay, Lord, please.*

The second time this happened, she spent almost two weeks in hospital and a number of different tests were carried out to try to diagnose what was happening. I couldn't cope with life during this time; it was just all too much for me and I felt like I was a bad mother and that I was neglecting Lourdes.

I remember feeling like a zombie. I couldn't sleep or eat properly. The consultant paediatrician assigned to La Belle was very worried about me. I remember him asking if I was alright because I didn't look well. He felt it would do me some good to speak to someone. He referred me to see a counsellor.

I went downstairs to see the therapist and when I arrived there was a middle-aged man sitting in a room staring at me with a quizzical look on his face. I sat down while he introduced his name and job title and I froze. He wasn't a counsellor, he was a psychiatrist. All I remembered thinking to myself at this point was *Fuck, he's going to think I'm crazy and take my kids away. Right, the best thing to do right now is to pretend that I'm fine so he doesn't take my twins.*

But as I started to speak and tell him what happened to La Belle I broke down. I was sobbing uncontrollably and I'm sure what I was saying did not make any sense to him at the time.

At the end of our conversation he said, "Mrs Huie-Ajibola, I think you're in desperate need of some support at home. I can see you're struggling especially with what happened to your daughter. I'm going to write to your doctor about the conversations we've had and suggest you be referred to a counsellor to help with your anxiety. My job as a psychiatrist is to assess psychological problems that people might be experiencing. In some cases they're sectioned to receive the care and treatment needed for their condition in case they're at risk of harming themselves or others, but I can see that's not the case with you. You've clearly had a very traumatic experience and seem to be suffering from postnatal depression, possibly along with an acute psychotic break."

I remember this conversation like it was yesterday; his words have always remained with me, I'd never experienced anything like this before. I stared at him after he had finished talking. I thought, *what on earth is this guy talking about, a psychotic break?*

I felt a huge sense of relief that my babies weren't going to be taken away from me, but then it occurred to me that I was going through a lot at that moment. I now had:

- Generalised Anxiety Disorder.
- Obsessive Compulsive Disorder.
- Newborn twins.
- Postnatal depression.
- Experienced a psychotic break.
- A poorly twin daughter.
- A dodgy right hip.
- De Quervains tenosynovitis in my left hand.
- A C-section scar taking ever so long to heal.

How the hell I am supposed to cope with all this? Maybe I should take some prescribed drugs; it might help me to deal with it all?

When La Belle was discharged from hospital the second time, she was given an appointment to have an impediment study. This examination measures the frequency and length of times a child refluxes over a 24 hour period.

This procedure involved a probe being inserted through La Belle's nostrils and pushed down until it rested at the lower end of her oesophagus where it joined the stomach. The outside cord was then attached to a little portable machine she had to wear as a rucksack on her back which recorded the level of reflux. When this procedure was carried out La Belle started screaming and crying; she wouldn't stay still which was standard for a baby only a few months old.

The doctor did explain it was an uncomfortable procedure—putting a probe down a baby's nose—but my husband wanted the procedure stopped as La Belle looked so distressed and in pain. Josh was very distraught by this, so much so he walked out of the medical room.

Once the probe was inserted and taped to La Belle's nose to keep it secure, I called Josh back into the room so that we could be shown by the doctor how to record any symptoms she had during the 24 hour period. The results from the study showed that Bella had Gestational Oesophageal Reflux Disorder (GORD), a condition in which milk can get stuck in the windpipe causing you to stop breathing.

I felt sad for her, but also relieved now that I finally had a diagnosis and was informed as to how to treat the condition. My anxiety didn't stop there though. Every time La Belle slept, I didn't. I was so fearful and scared she wouldn't wake up. I watched her sleep during the day, afternoon and night. I constantly worried about her every time she coughed or sneezed. I just couldn't help myself. I wasn't sleeping, eating or resting, which led to me having an emotional breakdown.

Fast forward to a few weeks later, I started my therapy sessions again, which was the best thing for me during this stressful time. I received support from my health visitor who referred me back to the same counselling service I used during my pregnancy which was part of my local hospital NHS trust. My therapist was my saviour. She was brilliant, understanding, non-judgemental and provided useful advice.

I explained what had been happening since the twins arrived including La Belle's health problems. She couldn't believe I had been through so much in such a short space of time. I was able to reintroduce what I learnt through CBT, which helped me to cope mentally and emotionally as a parent.

In researching anxiety disorders online and reading the booklets my therapist provided, I found that so many women suffer from anxiety and/or postnatal depression and go undiagnosed.

I used the following websites:

- www.mind.org.uk
- www.postpartum.net
- www.anxietyuk.org.uk

If you are reading this, have newborns and feel a little overwhelmed with everything, I sincerely urge you to seek professional advice—spotting these things is not always easy—sometimes your doctor might not recognise what you have, leaving you undiagnosed and unable to cope with life.

Sometimes it can be hard to see there is something wrong, but try to speak up and avoid suffering in silence. Don't feel embarrassed, ashamed or uncomfortable talking about your problems. Ask for help! There is a lot of support available for mothers and fathers suffering from anxiety.

If you require more in-depth information about the different types of anxiety, and for support with these conditions, please refer to the list of websites I've provided in the index of this book.

Survival tips for anxiety disorders

Claire from Essex, UK.
Mother of twin boys aged seven.

"I suffered from anxiety during my pregnancy and after giving birth, and still have it now. It is manageable for me but it's there, always. To cope I would look up information online on how to deal with certain situations i.e. sickness. I would advise you talk to someone if you have it; don't deal with it on your own. I also received support from my friends and family, which was helpful."

Jaikisbell from Ohio, USA.
Mother of twins, one boy and one girl aged eight months.

"My anxiety started at 24 weeks. That's when my waters ruptured; the reason I ended up in the hospital. I was hospitalised for a full month because of the high risk of delivering early and possible infection. I remember being in the hospital room, pregnant and alone most of the time because my husband had to work and my oldest son (seven years old) was at school. I was lonely. I had a therapist come in every day to check on me and make sure I was okay.

After the traumatic birth of my twins I was in a difficult position because they were born prematurely and my little girl was not doing well. I was obsessed with blaming myself for the way the babies were born. When the doctor told me that my daughter wouldn't make it past her first day of life, I was so angry, not only at myself, but angry at the doctors, and all I did was cry. I stayed with the twins, and I wanted nothing to do with my family. My husband was my rock, and to be honest he put up with a lot of my mood swings, anger and emotional outbursts. He really did most of the work around the house and once I crumbled, he just said that he was right there for me for whatever I needed. We did counselling, and I was put on antidepressants for three months. I still talk to my therapist, but I am no longer on medication. I am grateful that I held on to hope, my daughter is doing so much better now.

If you experience anxiety during pregnancy or after childbirth, I would advise you to take deep breaths, and take it one day at a time. Lean on your partner, family and friends for support if you have them and remember you are not alone. I had my husband who was my go-to person. The Neonatal Intensive Care Unit (NICU) nurses also were amazing and gave me suggestions and lots of information on how to deal with my anxiety, which helped."

Suzanne from London, UK.
Mother of twin boys aged six.
"I experienced anxiety towards the end of my pregnancy, around 32 weeks; it was an overwhelming feeling of worry and anxiousness. It also continued after the twins were born and didn't really go away until they started school, as I constantly worried about their wellbeing.

To start with I didn't realise I had anxiety. I didn't know what was happening to me. I just knew I felt different and it wasn't a nice feeling. Once I was aware of it, I did things differently to help cope with it. For example, when going out I planned my journeys to avoid feeling anxious. I had to thoroughly organise myself in advance to try and prevent situations that would make me feel anxious.

I would highly advise you talk to someone about how you are feeling; don't hold it in. There is help available to you. I spoke with my doctor who was very helpful and supportive. I was referred for counselling, to talking therapy and I had CBT, which did help me cope with the anxiety. I would definitely recommend this. I mainly received support from my GP and therapist, and I read information online and downloaded mindfulness meditations. I read a self-help book which was really useful."

Kris from California, USA.
Mother of triplets, two boys and one girl aged two.
"Anxiety was a big part of our lives around the time we started planning to have children. We had five miscarriages before having IVF. My husband and I were both very anxious when I fell pregnant with triplets because we constantly worried about whether they would be okay. The anxiety was intense throughout. And it didn't stop there. When the triplets were born (at 30 weeks and six days), they were transferred to the Neonatal Intensive Care Unit (NICU).

This was extremely hard on my husband and I, especially because our triplets came home at different times. Triplet one came home after 39 days, Triplet two at 41 days and Triplet three at 56 days. We had two boys and one girl. Our daughter spent the longest time in the NICU and I wasn't allowed to stay overnight with her at the hospital, which was heart breaking.

I struggled to cope with anxiety; it was very hard. I had therapy when I miscarried but that didn't help me. So, when pregnant with triplets, I was apprehensive about therapy again. I just dealt with it my own way. I didn't see a therapist but spoke to one occasionally, who was based on the NICU ward of the hospital for the benefit of all parents.

I also had a lot of anxiety when I didn't return to work. I felt like I'd lost my independence and didn't have that income I was used to having. I would most definitely advise all new parents suffering from anxiety to talk to someone. Don't keep it to yourself; it's important that you take care of you, so you can take care of your children. There is support available. I had support from my husband and my mum, and we hired a 'mother's helper' to support us with cleaning, doing the laundry and feeding babies. That extra set of hands made a huge difference."

Debora from London, UK.
Mother of twin boys aged seven.
"I suffered from anxiety, which was based around the babies being healthy and not premature. I worried about this but to cope I used a lot of healing techniques such as meditation and Reiki, which really worked well for me. I would advise you to take each moment at a time. Reward yourself and know that you are not alone. I received support and help from my support groups and friends. If you can do the same, they can really help."

Rebecca from Northamptonshire, UK.
Mother of twin girls aged one.
"My partner and I were anxious as twin parents but mainly over the worry of sleep, or lack of it, because of having two babies to care for at the same time. Our twins were our first children together and a surprise pregnancy. I have two children from a

prior relationship and my partner has three children from his prior relationship. We gained support from each other mainly because the second you tell anyone you're having twins, they react negatively with comments such as, "Twins, how will you cope?" and "Double trouble," which isn't helpful. No one ever asked how we felt about it. I struggled a lot with my hormones, birth control and the disappointment of an early birth and leaving hospital empty-handed as they were nine and a half weeks early and had to go into the Neonatal Intensive Care Unit (NICU)."

Those feelings of anxiousness, worry and fear can sometimes get the better of us whether it's before or after giving birth, as explained above by some of the parents. We want the best for our children, but with that there sometimes comes an overwhelming sense of wanting to make sure our children are safe and secure, and that we, as parents, are doing the best we can to provide for them.

However, what we also need to ensure is that we, as parents, are also looking after ourselves. Our own health and wellbeing is paramount. I am a true believer in self-care. If you are struggling with anxiety as an expectant mum or post-pregnancy mum or dad, there is no harm or shame in seeking support and advice to help you cope, especially during such an overwhelming time in your life.

As previously mentioned I had CBT with my therapist, which was beyond useful for me especially because of how I was feeling before and after pregnancy—what a huge transition! My therapist informed me there are many ways to treat an anxiety disorder and one way that really worked well for me was writing down my worries and fears in a notebook. This helped me to reflect and cope with parenthood much better because I would read back what I had written about a feeling or experience. I encourage you to try it too. Be honest and truthful about how you feel. Use a pencil so you can reuse pages if you like. Write it down, let it out and reflect.

My Notes

How are you feeling? Make some notes here and remember to take time to stop and reflect.

"When in doubt, choose kids. There will be plenty of time later to choose work."

-Anna Quindlen-

CHAPTER FOUR

Returning to Work

There are so many benefits to having a job—working as part of a team or on your own, as part of an organisation or your own business. Having a job can offer a purpose, tap into a passion, it boosts your sense of self-worth, provides independence, can make you new friends, and for most of us, the most important factor is that it helps you to provide for your family. For parents, so many say that going to work is easier than staying at home in that first year... for many of us work is an escape route from being with your children 24/7!

Not that I'm saying that we don't enjoy being with them, but more that we all need a break and a change of scenery sometimes. This chapter focuses on returning to work after maternity or paternity leave—drawing on my own experience. It includes how best to prepare for the return, whether you are excited to be returning or feeling a bit anxious about the change.

Following is a list of how you might be thinking and feeling about entering the world of work again as a new mum with dependents to care for:

- Where has the time gone?
- I can't believe it's gone so quickly.
- I don't want to go back to work.
- OMG! I can feel the anxiety kicking in.
- I can't wait to go back to work.
- I am so excited to be returning to work.
- I need some me time.
- Looking forward to some adult conversation.
- Time to change my routine to meet work-life balance commitments.
- Who is going to look after my children? I need childcare.
- How expensive is childcare?
- I need to reduce my working hours.
- Can I work flexibly?
- I don't want to feel overwhelmed.
- I need some structure in my life.
- How will I plan all of this?

As parents we know returning to work after having children can be challenging. For some of us, maternity leave goes very quickly and for others slowly, but one thing I think we all have in common is that overwhelming feeling of change. It can be a major transition to get back into the routine of work-life balance, especially when you have dependants who rely on you.

As my maternity time was coming to an end, I felt the time away from work had gone very quickly and I didn't want to go back to work just yet, but at the same time I felt eager to return to having some time to be focus on my career. I also wanted a break from my twins, as it was non-stop.

Work would be an outlet of downtime for me even though

my job was rather demanding. I knew I would enjoy not having to cook, clean and change nappies constantly and I really looked forward to having some adult conversation during the day, which I missed. So, looking back at the list above, I would definitely say that more than one of those thoughts applied to my life; in actual fact all of crossed my mind at some point. It was like a rollercoaster of emotions trying to think about all the things I needed to do before returning to work, when I was going to do them and how I was going to get them done.

Let's face it, the majority of us don't like change. When we are used to the way certain things are in our lives and something happens that causes transformation to take place, it can at times be quite challenging to cope with. This occurred with me as I started to think about returning to work and not being at home with my girls. It took longer than anticipated to adjust and, in hindsight, I think I went back to work too soon with my twins. I went back to work in July 2018, eight months after my twins had been born. It's different for everyone I realise but before I knew it I had to start putting things into place in preparation for returning to work – it takes time to get it all sorted. Most importantly I had to discuss childcare arrangements with my husband, which I left until quite late as I was overthinking all that needed to be done.

Ensuring you find suitable childcare that you are happy with can be time-consuming. Some parents decide to send their children to nursery once they return to work; others may choose to have an au pair or childminder. We spent some weeks at length searching for childcare. I enquired about childcare services in my area through the playgroup my children attended. I spoke to mums about their arrangements. I spoke to my health visitor who put me in contact with someone from my local borough's children's education services and received a list of nurseries and childminders locally. Lastly, we researched childcare providers online, organisations and independent providers.

I thought it would be beneficial for the girls to go to nursery, but my husband thought it was best that someone came to our home to look after them because they were so young. He felt it would be better for the twins to stay at home in their own environment and in familiar surroundings. It also meant we would not have to dress them for the day, prepare their bag and drop them off and pick them up during the week. When he explained this to me it made a lot of sense, especially as I started to think about the overwhelming reality of having to get them ready every morning (as well as getting myself ready) before work. No thanks!

So, we both came to an agreement that a childminder coming to us was best. In the process of searching for childcare online I came across a really good, well-recommended website called www.childcare.co.uk. They also have an App that you can download on your phone. I found a wide range of suitable childcare providers on there and after a few interviews, reference checks and observations of their interaction with the twins, we managed to find a great fit for us. It was someone who was also capable of working flexible hours to suit our working commitments. I actually felt a sense of relief that I could return to work with my children in safe hands during my absence.

It was a nostalgic feeling to be finally returning back to work as a school teacher where I could indulge in some adult conversation with my work colleagues instead of listening to baby babble all day.

I was due to return to work on Monday 4th June 2018. This was the least busiest time of the academic school year. It was the summer term. BTEC, GSCE and A-Level exams were coming to an end and there were fewer students in school.

My favourite time of the school year is the summer term. I love when it's bright outside all day long. My students are in a happier mood and it's nearing the end of the academic year.

However, this became short-lived. I remember the exact day like it was yesterday. It was when La Belle fell ill and was hospitalised, which meant I had to take additional time off work. I didn't return until a month later, in the middle of July, and only had a week left until the school year finished.

That week felt like the longest week of my life. I was constantly worried about La Belle and didn't want to leave her. Fortunately, I had time over the summer holidays to recuperate after such a traumatic event. When I returned to work in September for the beginning of the new school year I felt more confident, less anxious and ready to start my life as a working mum.

The twins were 20 months old, growing fast and learning how to be more independent. Lourdes had already started to walk and explore her surroundings and La Belle's health had improved.

However, a month after returning to work we had to find new childcare arrangements. This time it was even more challenging as I had less time to search for a replacement. I spoke to my cousin Caroline about our issues around finding suitable childcare and she mentioned our Aunty Emma might be able to help, as she was retired. So, I asked her and all our childcare problems were resolved in one call. Things were finally starting to look up.

I remember saying to my husband that I thought maternity and paternity rules and regulations for mums and dads returning to work needed to be changed for parents who had multiples. This might sound controversial, but I think parents with multiples should be entitled to additional time off work, especially dads, as their time is short enough as it is already with only two weeks off.

In most cases the mother is the main carer of a newborn as the infant requires breast milk, but bonding between your partner and child plays a key role in their growth and development, especially doing skin-to-skin. There just wasn't enough time for this and that's one of the things my husband said he wished he was able to do more of.

I have met plenty of mums that were very excited to return to work. Having that separation from home life for a few hours a day did them good and I agree based on my own experiences. For those hours at work I was "just" Leonie.

It's important that when you are planning to return to work to always prepare yourself mentally, so you're not overwhelmed. If you are in a demanding job, I would contact your employer to ask them what you might need to prepare before returning to work so you know what to expect. Also, if you are considering reducing the number of hours/days you work, discuss this with your employer well in advance so they can put measures in place to ensure this happens. This is something I did so I could spend more time with the twins.

Furthermore, if you are struggling at work because you're

trying to cope with this new transition, please don't suffer in silence: ask for help and support. It's important that you have organised childcare as it can take some time to get the right fit.

Top tips to help you return to work
Here are my top tips that worked for me when planning to return to work after maternity leave. I have also listed some useful websites with information about maternity and returning to work. This information will vary depending on the country you live in however I hope you find the tips below useful.

Working hours
If you are returning to work part-time inform your employer by giving them notice of this so they can make arrangements. Also consider your finances as your income will reduce once hours have been changed.

Plan and prepare
When you return to work there might be a few things you need at your disposal to help you ease back into the working environment.

- A photo of your babies.
- A mug for your tea/coffee.
- A reusable water bottle to keep you hydrated throughout the day.
- A breast pump if needed to express milk ready for home time, including a nursing pad and a decent bag to store all of this.

- A cushion for the chair at your desk. If you suffered from back problems during pregnancy this will help improve posture.

Find suitable childcare
Research online and contact your local area's children's education department. If you are going down the nursery route visit the nursery, research it online and ask other parents with children there what they think. If you are seeking a childminder or au pair, ensure you interview them and observe how they interact with your children. Most importantly follow up on the references they provide.

Look good, feel great
Avoid trying to squeeze into pre-pregnancy clothing.

For lots of mums it can take a little while to lose the weight gained during pregnancy, so purchase a few new items, treat yourself and remember to buy what you feel comfortable in that's also suitable for your place of work. Did you know it can take about six to 10 weeks for your uterus to go back to its original size after pregnancy? Don't be too hard on yourself.

Organise your home
If your children are being looked after in your home, organise some cupboard space so your childminder/au pair can access items for your children in one place. This will avoid them having to call you at work every five minutes to find things. Use your cupboard for your children's toiletries, blankets, sheets, extra clothes and toys etc.

Separation anxiety
It's pretty common for young children to experience separation anxiety if they are separated from their main carer. It's also something parents can experience too. Don't worry we all go through it but remind yourself that you'll see them again in a few hours.

Useful websites for information on maternity leave:
- www.citizensadvice.org.uk
- www.nct.org.uk
- www.acas.org.uk
- www.gov.uk
- www.moneyadviceservice.org.uk

Survival tips for returning to work

Ebony from London, UK.
Mother of twin girls aged nine.
"My twins were nine months when I returned to work full-time and that was a big challenge for me. Getting myself and them ready every morning was a lot of work; it took time to adjust but I got there in the end. In order to survive returning to work it's important you have a strict routine. Here's a tip —prepare your babies' bag the night before for nursery so you don't have to rush in the mornings. Routine was so important for me because it kept me sane. I didn't want to stress myself out, so I made sure I was organised."

Debora from London UK.
Mother of twin boys aged seven.
"Choose a good nursery for your children to attend. To ease into work-life balance, if you can, employ a cleaner to help at home, therefore when you return to work you don't have to worry about having to tidy up. Also, try to keep your children in a routine for night-time; this really worked well for me, as it helped my twins settle better for bedtime, which made the mornings more manageable."

Lesley from Scotland, UK.
Mother of triplet girls aged two.
"Although it can be daunting leaving your children for the first time, it really is so important to have adult interaction and switch your brain back on again. I became 'Lesley' again after returning to work. It allowed me to miss the kids and appreciate everything I had, as I quickly forgot all the stressful

moments. I looked forward to getting home to see them again. It made the time I did have of work more precious and I used it more wisely."

Lauren from Colorado, USA.
Mother to triplet, two girls and one boy aged two.
"I went on maternity leave quite early on in my pregnancy, as I ended up on strict bed rest from 16 weeks. When I eventually went back to work part-time my triplets were two years old. I work as a nurse and I was able to go back a couple times a month to keep my licence current and allow us to work out what the kinks were. My kids are almost three now and I still only work one day a week.

When returning to work, it's important you ease back in as best as you can. There will be changes in your life as a mum of multiple children so the best way to deal with them before returning to work would be to have a plan laid out that works for your household. Speak to your partner about what you need to make the transition back possible.

One thing that is hard that people don't think about is when your husband/partner goes back to work—they just do it. There isn't a process on how to deal with it, they just go back to work. So, when you are ready to go back to work, make sure you are both on the same page and able to divide up the responsibilities that you once solely held as a stay-at-home parent. We didn't have to worry about finding a childcare provider and interviewing; we already knew the person who was taking care of our kids. I didn't feel overwhelmed by being away from the triplets and I'm still their primary caregiver."

Claire from Essex, UK.
Mother of twin boys aged seven.
"When you return to work, try and get family and friends to help with childcare, if you can, to bring costs down. The best way to deal with change is to try to find a happy medium with your routine. This made me feel like I had a structure and that I was in control. When preparing yourself for returning to work it's best to be organised with pick-up and drop-off times. Really know your journey and give yourself ample time."

Shelby from Pennsylvania, USA.
Mother of triplets, two girls and one boy aged eight months.
"Our triplets were 10 weeks old when I went back to work. I work over 40 hours a week and my husband went back when they were three weeks old. I work a regular 8am to 4pm shift, and as soon as I get home he leaves for his shift and gets home at 10pm. It was hard coming home from work and knowing that 'work' was going to continue. It was especially difficult being by myself for the bath/bottle/night routine and to stay on schedule.

I don't have much free time in the evenings. As soon as I put the babies to bed I'm eating dinner alone, cleaning the house, trying to catch up on my workload that I had to bring home to finish, then I'm rushing to bed to try to get as much sleep as possible before the babies wake up again the next morning.

I would say it took about a week for both of us to get into a good day and night routine on our own. Absolutely practice your morning work routine prior to returning to work to time yourself and work out any errors. After your children are in bed, prepare for the next day. Lay out, make and prepare everything you'll need for the next day so there are fewer hiccups in the morning. Even the small things matter, such as having your hair curler laid out, coffee pot ready to go, and bottles ready with the tops off! Everything saves you time and equates to less stress."

One major thing each working mother needs to realise is that you are not choosing your career over your children. It is easy to get sad or mad that you may be missing milestones but providing for the needs of your family comes first. While you are home, ensure there are no distractions. Put your full focus on your kids and your marriage. Do not deviate from this at home, so you can be fully focused at work.

Returning to work can be daunting but it's also rewarding. As Deborah from London mentioned, routine is key. It will help you avoid those feelings of anxiousness, stress, dread and just being overwhelmed. Having multiples is already overwhelming—we don't need to add to that!

In Chapter two, I spoke about how organised I used to be before becoming a parent and once that happened my organisational skills went from 10 to zero in the space of a few weeks. I couldn't survive without my diary and everything I needed to do was written down or on my phone calendar, which promptly provided me with set reminders so I wouldn't forget anything.

My mission for returning to work was to be more organised to ensure I efficiently managed my work-life balance. There were a number of things I learnt during my first year of parenthood about how to survive returning to work and the most important lesson was letting go of trying to be perfect. You can't expect everything to be perfect all the time, although I did. Not being as organised as I used to be was an anxiety trigger for me, and when things went wrong, I went into panic mode because I did not know how to cope.

Perfection is non-existent with multiples; you cannot predict what life will be like on a day-to-day basis, so going with the flow can make your life so much easier. Yes, you can prepare for returning to work by having a good plan of what to do, but don't expect everything to be perfect. Just let go of the word perfect altogether: you'll do better without it in your vocabulary.

To help you effectively prepare for returning to work, use the space that follows to list all the things you need to do before the big day. This will ease any stress or anxiety you might be feeling about what needs to be put in place. You can always return to your list if you need to update it or make any changes, but I hope this helps you somewhat in the process of becoming a fully functioning working parent of multiples.

My Notes

Things to do before returning to work

1.

2.

3.

4.

5.

6.

7.

8.

9.

10.

11.

12.

"Communication is key, that's what counts."

-Leonie Huie-

CHAPTER FIVE

Date Night

It can only be a good thing to want to spend a bit of quality time with your partner, right? But when you are a new parent looking after newborn multiples, quality time can become something of a lost thought.

Date night with kids, what's that all about? Well, let me tell you. Date night is something couples do in their relationship as a way of spending some meaningful time together. Whether you have children or not, you may lead a busy life, sometimes not prioritising or having enough time for your partner, which can put a strain on your relationship. Making sure you and your partner put some special time aside for your relationship can be the key to its success. But for a new parent, date night might be the last thing on your mind because the only date you'll be thinking about is the one you have with your pillow! I'm pretty sure that most parents mainly think about sleep and only sleep in their first year of having multiples.

In this chapter I'll explain why I think date night is so important and why couples need to ensure they make time for one another to reconnect and remember who they are other than being parents. When I talk about date night with other parents of multiples, responses usually involve some or all of the following comments:

- "Date night, what's that?"
- "Oh, that sounds lovely."
- "Err, non-existent in a house of sleep deprivation."
- "Who is going to watch the kids?"
- "You're kidding me, right?"
- "I just don't have the physical energy to breathe, let alone go out."

I empathised with these responses and also found the amusing because they resonated with how I felt in that first year.

When parents have some rare time to themselves, they spend it sleeping, cooking, cleaning, washing clothes, ironing, catching up on work. Where is date night supposed to fit into all this? There are some parents who have managed a date or two during this eventful time, which really helped them reconnect as a couple and relax in other people's company without having to worry about their children.

Here's what a few of them said:

- "It was nice to talk about anything other than breast milk and nappies."
- "I dressed up, put my heels on and wore make-up for the first time in six months. I felt normal again."
- "We had a double date once with some friends, which was nice: great food, great wine, great company."
- "I remember having a nice cold beer, it felt good."

- "We both have big families with grandparents who live close by so we managed to go out quite a few times during the first year; it was great to spend some alone time with my wife."

I must admit, my husband and I weren't interested in date night during my first year of parenting. When we had any spare time we just wanted to relax. Now that my twins have passed their first year milestone, on reflection, I do believe date night with your partner is important for several reasons.

Finding time to simply talk to one another and reconnect can make your relationship stronger and keep that spark between the two of you alive. The demands of looking after multiple children can sometimes place a strain on you which can leave you feeling stressed and overwhelmed, so having your partner there to communicate your feelings will help you feel better within yourself.

If you have the support, it's important you try to go out as a couple; a change of scenery might just be what you both need. It can be a romantic dinner, a movie or just a walk: spending that quality time with your partner makes all the difference.

Knowing you have one another to rely on is key to any relationship, even more so when there are newborn children involved who require your undivided attention.

Josh and I often talked about date night during the first year of parenting and that's as far as we got most of the time. I would define date night for us as an evening in front of the TV with one child on each lap. Our date night included La Belle and Lourdes. We were just too tired to go anywhere and with Josh working long hours. He was exhausted.

So, it was a movie and takeaway for us and milk for the twins. However, there were some benefits to this as we got the opportunity to talk about everything and anything other than nappies, milk, feeding time, bedtime. You get the picture!

We also acknowledged that we hadn't spent much time together as couple so decided to plan a little holiday with the twins to Spain. We both felt we were in need of some sun, sand and sea, a well-deserved trip which I will explain in more detail in the chapter entitled Travelling With Multiples.

Whilst away on holiday we were able to celebrate our new role as parents, discuss the highs and lows of parenting, how quickly the twins were growing and developing into their own personalities (which are completely different to each other), and promising to make time to focus on each other a bit more, as well as enjoying one another's company.

Here are some common problems couples can face after giving birth

1. Ineffective communication

Communication is the most significant part of any relationship. If you can't communicate with your partner then what's the point in having a relationship? You should be able to share what's on your mind so you are both on the same page and it takes a lot of work to try to avoid any confusion or breakdown in communication.

During the first few months of our twins being born, communication between my husband and I was poor. We were basically living in the same house yet not speaking to each other much about anything other than feeding, changing or putting the twins to sleep.

I was going through a number of health problems including postnatal depression and Josh looked tired and gaunt all the time. I was concerned about his health and wellbeing as research shows a lack of sleep is linked to diabetes, heart disease, and obesity (www.nhs.uk) but I didn't feel as though there was anything I could do about it, as I had my own problems to deal with. This might sound selfish, but I could not physically, emotionally or mentally take on anything more than what I was already carrying. My plate was full; actually, my plate was overflowing. I did suggest he see a doctor, but he would always respond with, "I'm fine." I don't know what it was about him and avoiding doctors when he clearly needed some support, and due to the lack of communication between us, at that point the last thing on my mind was date night or trying to find time to spend with my husband.

Communication for us as a couple started to improve after three months and even more so when we went on our first family holiday. We also attended therapy sessions after La Belle was hospitalised. Even though the sessions were about me and how I was coping, they had a lot to do with home life, so his attendance was significant. Due to his working hours, Josh attended when he could, as he knew it was important to me. I think he realised the reality of me not coping when I first told him I would be having therapy sessions and I asked him to come with me. However, he wasn't expecting the therapist to ask him questions about how he was coping as a father of multiples; at first he was reluctant to answer but did open up to say the lack of sleep was unreal and he didn't expect it to be quite so bad. I found these sessions very helpful. I was able to talk about La Belle being ill, how parenthood affected me, my health and my wellbeing. Flipping heck, it sounds like a disease when I put it like this, but it was taking its toll on me physically, mentally, emotionally and socially. Yes, we were lucky to have a strong support network of people around us and yes, we could ask my family and friends for help when we needed it but I felt like my brain was going to explode with everything I was trying to deal with all at one time.

It's true when people say there is only so much a human being can take. When I explained how I was feeling to Josh he understood; he hadn't realised I was taking on so much and how mentally drained I was. We both agreed we would communicate better and tell each other if we needed help or support and this made our relationship more positive moving forward. We even found time to have a date night here and there through pre-planning and asking the twins' grandparents and my sisters to look after them.

Overall, positive communication is healthy for all relationships. Knowing how to communicate with your partner in a clear, honest, and mindful way is a tool you can use to help improve how you both feel, which will maintain a strong relationship during times of extreme challenge and/ or transformation.

2. Relationship mishaps

Being a new parent to multiples can take its toll on you and your partner, so having a strong relationship is important. This is a time where the bond between you needs to be stronger than ever. It's not just the physical support needed in helping with the cooking and cleaning but there's also the emotional support to consider as you both may experience times where parenthood can be rather overwhelming.

To help keep your relationship alive, try scheduling in some regular time together alone—as I mentioned earlier this can be at home or out on a date. The goal here is to improve the relationship you already have, to help you reconnect with one another and lean on each other when needed.

This is what Josh and I did after realising we never made time for each other due to being full-on with the twins. Once our levels of communication improved we made more of an effort to plan in advance some time alone like going out to our favourite restaurant or going to the cinema. Josh would occasionally buy me flowers, which was a nice gesture, and treated me to regular massages with the maternity masseuses I saw whilst pregnant—heaven on earth!

Josh paid more attention to how I was feeling which really helped our relationship and I sincerely appreciated the massages which relieved the tension and stress building up around my body. My masseuse always said I had a lot of tension in my upper back and shoulders, but after she went to work on my body I felt like a new women. I could think more clearly and always took the opportunity to go for a short walk after my massage just to get some fresh air and some well-deserved me time.

Josh knew this was something I needed to do for me, for my own sanity, and he was happy to help by looking after the twins. Him being supportive made me feel I could rely on him, more so than I was already. It left me with a feeling of warmth. This made me realise more than ever, if you are happy within the relationship you have with your partner, then this in turn will support you both in your new role as parents and in doing a better job so your children will feel even more loved than they already are.

3. Finances

According to Child Poverty Action Group in 2018, the average cost of raising a child in the UK (based on what the public thinks is a minimum standard of living) from newborn to 18 years old costs £150,753 (www.cpag.org.uk).

When I read this I thought to myself, *Okay, so I'll just go ahead and times that by two!*

This figure is an estimate so it could possibly be higher if you factor in additional activities and travelling abroad.

OMG! I'm screaming internally right now!

This leads on to my next common issue in relationships: finances. After childbirth, finances can be a bit of a struggle for some families. You might experience a reduction in the amount of income coming into your household because Mum is on maternity leave or Dad may have changed his hours.

It can feel like a bit of a lose/lose situation. The cost of having multiples truly does mount up. Your average household spending can double or triple, which can cause a lot of tension and arguments at home, leaving you with no quality time together let alone to go out for date night.

Even though I was on maternity leave, what I did as soon as I found out I was pregnant was saved a bit of money each month before the twins arrived. Luckily for us, we still had a good household income, but let me be clear, the cost of newborns is astronomical. For example, the amount of money for nappies, baby wash, baby cream, the list goes on and on, and we had to buy double everything. Parents who have triplets or more, I feel your pain.

In addition to this, our daughter La Belle had severe eczema. She received free prescribed medication from the doctor but as parents we were overly conscious of using steroid cream to treat her condition so we spent additional money buying natural remedies from our local health foods store such a aloe vera gel and lotion. We purchased Childs Farm products as well.

The cost for baby items do add up. To help ease some pressure with your finances, plan with your partner how to save some money before the babies arrive. We put a bit of money away each month before the twins arrived. You could also contact local charities or organisations that support families. They could provide financial help and support to those on low incomes.

4. Jealousy

I remember talking to a group of mums I met at a multiples playgroup about whether they have a date night with their partners and if they felt it was important to do so, and they all agreed it was important. Some wished they could have date night but just didn't have the time to organise it whereas others had family support to help look after their multiples when they went out.

One thing I remember that stuck with me after conversing with this group of mums was their partners feeling a bit jealous and left out because all Mum's time and energy went into looking after their children.

One mother said, "I read this could happen in relationships

with newborns, where the man feels the baby or babies are getting all the attention."

Another said, "I argue a lot with my husband because he felt neglected."

Some of the other women echoed this. I actually couldn't believe what I was hearing. I thought, *Surely this can't be a thing?*

Now, let me be clear, not all men feel like this. I may sound naïve, but I had no idea that *any* men felt this way!

I came across an article about men being jealous of their children on www.mumsnet.com. This is a very useful site full of information, tips and advice, created by parents, for parents.

I came across a thread about women who had partners who were jealous of their new baby taking up Mum's attention, leaving no time for them. Dads would feel excluded and unwanted.

This got me thinking about my husband and how he felt about all the times I spent focused on the twins instead of him and our conversation went something like this:

"Josh, I know the twins are eight months old now, but have you ever felt a bit jealous that I spend more time with them instead of with you?"

"What are you on about? Isn't that what's supposed to happen?"

"Yes, but I just wanted to ask you because I've never asked you this before. I was reading a thread online about mums having problems with their jealous husbands," I said.

"Why are they jealous?" Josh asked.

"Well, the women online were discussing that their husbands and partners were jealous of the time they spent with their newborn which left them feeling neglected, lonely and isolated."

"What? Why would they be jealous of their own children, that doesn't even make any sense to me. Honestly, it's not an issue for me. All I want in my life right now is to catch up on some sleep. I'm beyond sleep deprived! No time for jealously, just sleep!"

I thought he might say something like this, but I just wanted to be sure he didn't feel any resentment towards his children. Josh often spoke of sleep or the lack thereof throughout the first year of our twins' lives. We did have occasional moments where we spent time together cooking or lounging on the sofa, but they were rare earlier on. When our twins reached nine or 10 months old, we had a bit more time for ourselves.

Before we had the twins, once a week Josh and I would ensure we watched our favourite property development programme together along with a nice meal. That was our thing! However, when the twins came, we didn't watch it for over a year. Looking back, I think we only had date night a handful of times in our first year of parenting.

I do remember my mother and sister having our girls for a weekend so Josh and I could have a spa weekend away which was amazing. Yes, we managed to accomplish a 'Date Weekender' as I like to call it. We finally got some proper sleep and indulged in some pampering and it felt good. We felt like human again. However, we felt rather guilty when we collected the twins from my family because my mother and sister looked like *they* hadn't slept in a week. Oh yes, we knew that feeling all too well.

Towards the end of our twins' first year, we managed to have more quality time together. It took us planning in advance and arranging childcare. We both felt less stressed and finally got a little more sleep. Josh no longer walked around the house looking like the walking dead and I was able to regularly comb my hair and not have five-minute showers due to one of the twins waking up or crying.

I don't know what it was about our girls, but they always wanted our attention. Whenever we wanted to shower, eat, get dressed or just sit down for five minutes to have a cup of tea, they would demand to be held. It was like they knew we were desperate to have time away from them.

I remember asking my friends and family, "When on earth do things start to get a bit easier with kids?"

They would always say, "When they start to walk and talk, when they can feed themselves and dress themselves," but I beg to differ.

By the time our twins could walk they started to touch everything! It was yet another challenge for us as parents that we had to take on, and saying, "Don't touch that" was a complete and utter waste of our time. Although, one nice thing about the twins becoming more independent was that Josh and I were able to have more time for us.

Following, I have provided a list of my date night ideas, involving some form of communication which is key to any relationship with or without kids. Please try some of these if you get chance to spend some quality time together in your first year as multiple parents.

Date night ideas

Staying indoors	Going out
Ordering takeaway	Meal for lunch/dinner
Cooking a special meal	Cinema
Watching a movie	Bowling
Playing board games	Theatre
Having friends over	Take a walk
Enjoying an indoor picnic	Karaoke
Talking about 'the good old days'	Spa day/night

Survival tips for finding time for date night

Josh from London, UK.
Father of twin girls aged two.

"My wife and I liked the idea of date night which we thought was important in our first year of parenting but we spent most of it indoors. However, we did manage to go away for a spa weekend break which was exactly what we needed after my wife experienced a tough pregnancy. However, I think if you don't want to go out, then you can simply have date night in your living room with a movie and a takeaway. If you and your partner are spending quality time together and feeling less stressed and more relaxed, it doesn't matter where you spend date night."

Afia from London, UK.
Mother of twin girls aged three.

"We felt date night was important but we were realistic parents and cool with staying indoors. I think that's why we both liked routine, so that we could have some decent time to ourselves every evening. As new parents it's okay if you don't have time or the inclination for date night. The time will come to have that. Just make sure you communicate. Let each other know if you're struggling or you need some time alone. Have a lie in and don't begrudge each other for it. This's what's most important."

Suzanne from London, UK.
Mother of twin boys aged six.

"My husband and I felt date night was important but honestly, we didn't have time for it as much as we would have loved to.

We weren't able go out as we didn't have anyone to look after our twins and two other children so instead we had date night indoors, a few times during the first year of being parents. We cooked together, had a nice meal and played card games together and talked which was nice. You're not just a parent, you're a person too, who needs to wind down occasionally.

I think there are benefits to date night. It's important in a relationship as it helps to keep the relationship alive. With your partner try to talk about anything other than the everyday cooking, cleaning, bottle feeding and other housework duties. Another benefit of date night is you have one another to rely on and support; working together as a team makes the relationship and family stronger, so I would recommend it if you're able to do it."

Paul-Michael from London, UK.
Father of twin girls aged three.
"I think it's very important to have date night in the first year of parenting. I highly recommend it. We had our first date night when our twins were three months old. We ended up going for a meal not too far from home, but it was nice to get out of the house, enjoy different scenery and spend some quality time with my wife. I think there are benefits to date night, such as being able to communicate and talk with your partner more freely without interruptions, build on the relationship as a couple and discuss the future of your family. Some tips I would suggest for date night would be to do things together that you did when you were dating and never stop communicating with one another, regardless of how tough things might get. There's nothing like quality time together;

this could be on a couples retreat for example, where you get to unwind and reconnect."

Cassie from London, UK.
Mother of twin boys aged eight.

"Date night didn't happen for us due to it being full-on with the twins during their first year. We also had a four-year-old daughter at that time. During the first year of parenting I had a lot of health issues with my spine as well as carpel tunnel syndrome, which is a condition with your hands, causing severe pain, numbness and tingling. It was so bad I couldn't carry the twins for a short period of time so going out was not much of a priority. The closest we got to date night was when the kids were asleep, and we chilled on the sofa watching TV. However, I do think date night is important in a relationship. It helps to keep the relationship alive. If you can you should try to go out with your partner so you can both spend some quality time together, even if it's just for a few hours."

Leandra, from New York.
Mother of twin girls aged two.

"When the sum of your personal life is no longer just your partner, and you maintain a career, it's very easy to get caught up in or distracted by this new variable (your children!) and de-prioritise your relationship. You can't just rely on the simple fact that you love each other to carry you through. In my experience, date night has served as a reminder of who we both are in spite of having children. We incurred so many changes, both psychologically and environmentally, in that first year of marriage and if nothing else, date night facilitated an open forum to express these changes to each other. Like a sort of checks and balances, and we're still growing in the same direction which is important.

If you are a parent who is uncomfortable leaving your kids for too long, one thing that worked for my husband and I was going to dinner very early, about 5.30pm, and getting home just in time for bed time so we could tuck the kids in and then resume our alone time from home."

Well, the consensus here regarding date night is that yes, it is important to spend time with your partner, but you don't have to leave your house to spend quality time together, which is absolutely fine. I'm sure most people with newborn multiples would love to be able to go out for a meal, watch a movie or even have a picnic, but all of these things can be done at home too.

The most important thing about date night, I believe, is not so much about the date, it's about you as a couple finding time for each other, communicating effectively, being there for each other when things get tough, and being able to rely on one another for emotional support and wellbeing. I think the wording is all wrong—'date night' should just be called 'quality time' because when your children are under one, you tend to spend most of your time with them. Therefore, try to organise yourself effectively so that you and your partner can indulge in one another at home, but if you get the chance to embrace the outdoors, seize the moment.

I have provided some space on the next page for you to plan some quality time (date nights) together, whether inside or outdoors. As parents we know nothing is set in stone with little ones so use this as a rough guide and reschedule when needed.

My Notes

Option 1
What to do/where to go?

Stay home/go out?

For how long?

Who has the kids?

Option 2
What to do/where to go?

Stay home/go out?

For how long?

Who has the kids?

My Notes

Option 3

What to do/where to go?

Stay home/go out?

For how long?

Who has the kids?

Option 4

What to do/where to go?

Stay home/go out?

For how long?

Who has the kids?

"You know, it's so easy to be hard on yourself."

-Angela Bassett-

CHAPTER SIX
Postnatal Depression

That overwhelming feeling, the dread, tiredness, lack of interest, sadness, those endless tears, anxiousness, low mood and lack of sleep.

- "Why am I feeling like this?"
- "What's wrong with me?"
- "I just can't cope!"

When you have endless mixed emotions after giving birth the last thing on your mind is thinking you have postnatal depression (PND). Most mums don't even know they have it, but what they do know is they don't feel right, something's off, and then they put it down to childbirth when in actual fact it's more than that.

This chapter is about postnatal depression and the symptoms of this condition, as well as the treatment available to mums who have it. I have also provided the different steps I took to deal with my PND, which aided in improving my health and wellbeing. If you are pregnant or in your first year of parenting this is a very important read with the intention of providing you with some useful information and tools.

Worldwide, about 10% of pregnant women and 13% of women who have just given birth experience a mental disorder, primarily depression (www.who.int). Postnatal depression is a medical condition that usually affects women the first couple of weeks after giving birth; but you can experience PND months after giving birth or even a year later

Postnatal depression can also affect fathers and partners during and after pregnancy with one in 10 dads-to-be becoming depressed during their partner's pregnancy. When you have postnatal depression you can feel excessively tired, have severe anxiety and panic attacks, find it difficult to bond with your baby and feel as though you are not a good mother. In some cases you can experience recurrent thoughts of death or suicide. These overwhelming mixed feelings are rather common (www. pampers.co.uk).

During the first few days after giving birth some women experience a change in hormones which can lead to feeling depressed and emotional. This is called the 'baby blues.' You may have heard of this term. It only lasts up to a couple of weeks after childbirth and can cause a great deal of stress to a new mother.

However, there is a big difference between PND and the baby blues so let's not confuse the two. If you are experiencing any of the signs of PND two weeks after giving birth then it's very important you seek medical advice (www.tommy.org).

I wish I'd known this when I gave birth because I experienced symptoms of PND which lasted for months, but I wasn't aware I had it. I just thought the different feelings I was experiencing were down to having twins and struggling to cope especially due to the lack of sleep.

There are many symptoms of PND that you can experience which I have listed below:

- Low mood.
- Unwarranted crying.
- Difficulty bonding with your baby.
- Eating more than usual.
- Overwhelming fatigue or loss of energy.
- Reduced interest and pleasure in activities you used to enjoy.
- Feeling angry and irritable.
- Severe anxiety and panic attacks.
- Withdrawing from loved ones.
- Loss of appetite.
- Worry that you're not a good mother.
- Feelings of worthlessness, guilt, shame or inadequacy.
- Insomnia.
- Feeling sleepy during the day.
- Difficulty focusing.
- Decreased ability to handle everyday tasks.
- Thoughts of harming yourself or your baby.
- Recurrent thoughts of death or suicide.

In researching the different symptoms of PND that mothers experience, I was quite surprised at how extensive the list was. This condition also affects women differently especially if you have other health-related issues like I did. When I look back at this list I know why I was feeling so overwhelmed. I was already dealing with anxiety and obsessive compulsive disorder well before I was pregnant. In addition to this, I incurred hip problems which led to me being on crutches for the last few months of my pregnancy. Lastly, I had to deal with the pain from having a caesarean. Oh my, was the aftermath of a C-section excruciatingly painful. I experienced a lot of itching, which was bizarre to me until the nurse explained it was common after having a C-section.

After giving birth and being checked by all the doctors, nurses, midwives and other healthcare professionals—who I must say were remarkably helpful, caring, kind and supportive people – the aching, the throbbing, the tenderness in my stomach was hell on earth! All I wanted was pain relief.

"Please just drug me up, I'm begging you," I heard myself saying to the nurse in charge of administering my pain medication.

She explained that they had to lower my dosage as I would be breastfeeding.

"But you can't leave me feeling like this! How can I breastfeed in pain?" I asked.

"Let the pain meds start working. I've just given them to you, it won't be long now. Also, you need to try and walk around a bit to exercise your legs; you don't want your body feeling stiff from lying in a hospital bed."

At this point it was like the pain suddenly stopped! I was stuck on what the nurse had just said to me.

"Monique, did she just say to try and walk? She must be insane, right? Walk where? I just want drugs. She can't be serious," I said to my younger sister, who insisted I at least try. "But I don't want to try, Mon. I just want drugs.! Can you ask her if I can have some more drugs? She might listen to you."

At that point Monique just gave me a quizzical look. Need I say more?

I have to say the nurses were so patient and tolerant with me; all I could think about was drugs, not breast milk. However, once the medication eventually started to work I felt so much better. The pain had subsided, but I was still left with:

- Anxiety.
- Obsessive compulsive disorder.
- Hip problems.
- Itching around my C-section scar.
- Postnatal depression—now added to the list.

By the time I was discharged from hospital to go home, honestly I didn't feel happy or excited. I wanted all the nurses and doctors to come with me. Panic mode set in yet again; the realisation that I had to deal with motherhood alone without them was frightening. Yes, I had my husband, family and friends to support me, but I wanted the nurses and doctors too. I felt as though I wasn't ready to take this new role on.

Have you ever had an out-of-body experience? Like you had no control over your body? Have you ever had trouble bonding with your child just days after giving birth? Well, I scored a hat-trick there. I experienced all three and during this time I had no idea what the hell was happening to me.

After returning home from the hospital with two babies in tow, I felt low, had a lack of energy, was tired, had low self-esteem, withdrawn and experienced difficulties bonding with La Belle and Lourdes. Honestly, I thought this was normal after childbirth due to the physical trauma women experience with their bodies, but when I felt like I couldn't bond with my newborn twins I knew something wasn't right.

I remember feeling like my body wasn't mine. I couldn't do anything with it. I was visibly there but not in spirit. I was functioning properly and disconnected from myself. This may sound insane to you, but it happened. My body wasn't doing what I wanted it to. I had no control over it, and I didn't know why. I didn't share this information with anyone at the time, not even my husband. I wasn't sure what was happening to me and thought it would just pass.

And then came the bonding, or lack of it. I remember feeling scared holding both my girls together. My midwives encouraged my husband and I to do skin-to-skin which I struggled with at first. I just couldn't bond with the twins and this really upset me. I would watch our daughters lying on daddy's chest all cosy, looking adorable, and would think to myself, *Why can't I do that? Why is that so difficult for me?*

I found myself crying a lot and I held in the tears around my friends and family because I didn't want them asking me questions. My husband never knew what I was going through at the time because I kept it from him. I just didn't want anyone to know.

These mixed feelings I was having got even worse when it came to breastfeeding the twins. I remember breastfeeding for the first time and experiencing the most excruciating pain in my stomach. I thought, *What the fuck is that awful pain?* And the pain only happened when I breastfed. My midwives explained that it was normal and it was my stomach muscles contracting due to breastfeeding.

"The more you breastfeed, the more it helps your stomach to shrink," the midwife said.

What an incentive, I thought. *You get to feed your children and get back into shape at the same time without going to the gym. Double bonus!*

Unfortunately the incentive didn't work for me because I found it very difficult to breastfeed. La Belle couldn't latch on which really made the process challenging for me. I also couldn't deal with the stress of trying to get her to latch on. It made me anxious, and I was frightened that I would hurt her in the process of trying to position her correctly to breastfeed.

Lourdes on the other hand was able to latch on straight away but I felt so uncomfortable with feeding her. When the midwives first demonstrated how to breastfeed, I thought it was quite aggressive the way mums are expected to hold their babies' necks and force the nipple into their mouths, which scared me. The midwives explained that I wasn't hurting my children; instead I was teaching them to find my nipple and feed automatically (I still beg to differ). This just didn't work for me, and I was worried I was starving my twins so I went from expressing milk to formula milk as I just couldn't bond with them through feeding.

My feelings of low mood, lack of energy and tiredness went on for a few months. Luckily the challenges I faced with bonding improved as soon as I started bottle feeding. After starting therapy the second time I read online that postnatal depression can start at any time in the first year of childbirth, but for me it started at the beginning. I just never knew I had it.

It's a common problem, affecting more than one in every 10 women in the UK (www.nhs.uk). Women can feel a range of emotions in their first year of parenthood but there are ways to help treat PND that will make you feel better about yourself, improve your health and wellbeing.

As a PND sufferer I would highly advise you share with those close to you how you are feeling or speak with a medical professional. I didn't realise I had PND until La Belle fell ill at eight months and I had to see a psychiatrist. He felt that I was showing common signs of PND. I went months without help or support because my midwives, doctor and health visitor did not realise what I had.

There is a lot of support available for parents online through articles, blogs, podcasts, YouTube videos and support groups/ communities on social media platforms such as Facebook and Twitter. You can also receive support and advice from your doctor who will be able to refer you to additional services/ groups that can help you. Try not to do what I did and not tell anyone. I honestly believe I would have coped better if I opened up about how I was feeling after giving birth.

Nonetheless, even though I hadn't told anyone about the symptoms I was experiencing at the beginning of my pregnancy, I was so determined not to let how I felt take over my life. I had a number of mixed emotions that I was dealing with and at times I felt like I was battling against myself and how I felt. Seeking medical attention would have been the best option here but I wasn't thinking about this at the time. It was a real struggle.

When the twins reached eight months old I started to feel better and have more energy. I actually ate whole meals and finally got my appetite back. I was more focused. I could complete daily tasks including housework and the crying stopped. I no longer felt angry or irritable.

There are treatments available for PND which mainly comes in these three forms:

- Therapy.
- Medication.
- Self-help strategies.

I decided to use therapy and self-help strategies and this was for a number of reasons. I like talking so when I was referred to therapy I had no issues with opening up about how I felt. I was offered medication by my doctor but decided to take the homeopathic route which I felt best suited my needs and my situation. However, if you feel medication is best suited to you it's important you seek medical advice from your doctor who would be able to assess your situation to help meet your needs.

I'm going to share with you some of the approaches I took to help improve and treat my postnatal depression, which also assisted in the improvement of my health and wellbeing holistically.

Step one
I had positive affirmations that I said to myself. This wasn't daily, but I said them as often as I could, especially when I was feeling negative about myself. The aim was to think more positively and provide myself with the empowerment I needed to feel better and to improve my emotional wellbeing. Here is what I said to myself:

- "Things will get better, they can't get worse."
- "You're doing a great job, the best you can do."
- "I love my girls, to the moon and back."

Did this work for me? Absolutely!

To be honest I didn't think it would, and just to be clear I didn't start to feel positive straightaway. It did take a few weeks, but nonetheless, I did start to feel better so I kept at it.

Consistency is key. Find time to ensure you do it. When you don't feel like doing it, reminding yourself of the benefits of this. It does work—be patient.

Step two

I drank plenty of water to keep myself hydrated throughout the day and night, especially because I lost my appetite. My husband would regularly buy me bottles of water and made sure that drank it.

You might think drinking water is not a big deal, but it's an integral part of everyone's diet, with the human body being made up of about 60% of it. Regardless of your age, sex or size, we all need to drink water and it's recommended by health professionals that we should drink two litres of water a day. Here are some of the benefits:

- Drinking water can improve our brain function and energy levels as it helps to keep our body hydrated.
- Drinking water boosts skin health because dehydration can make our skin more vulnerable to wrinkles and other skin-related issues.

- Drinking water can contribute to weight loss because it boosts our metabolic rate.
- Drinking water may help to treat and prevent headaches as dehydration can cause headaches and migraines.

Step three

I continued to do skin-to-skin with the twins at least once a day which I had struggled with but I eventually started to enjoy it as I felt less anxious and stressed. It melted my heart feeling their heartbeats on my chest, and I fell in love with their baby smell, their little hands and their little feet. During skin-to-skin I would quietly play my Norah Jones, Alicia Keys and Lauryn Hill albums in the background, which really helped me to relax throughout this bonding time with the girls. I also noticed they felt relaxed too as the music helped to soothe them. Even though my girls were approaching nine months and skin-to-skin is often carried out when babies are newborn, I still do it now and my girls love it.

Step four

I did some meditation at home for 30 minutes a couple of times a week when I had the opportunity to do so. This mainly happened when the girls were asleep. I would put on a short YouTube video (there are plenty to choose from) and lie on my yoga mat for 30 minutes. Once I finished the video I could feel the benefits straightaway. I felt much more calm, relaxed and less stressed. My anxiety and emotions were more controlled. Who knew how profound inhalation and exhalation could be? I would then join the girls for some sleep which I was in serious need of.

Step five

I went for short walks to the park and back sometimes with the twins and sometimes alone. I indulged in the fresh air and some mild exercise as I was still healing from my C-section. The walks really did me some good. I remember the nurse in the hospital telling me to keep my joints moving to avoid getting stiff, so walking for me was important. I also had problems with my right hip which I didn't want to get any worse. I would walk for about half an hour to an hour a few times a week which also gave me the opportunity to clear my head, think more positively and do something other than cooking, cleaning and ironing. Walking really helped to improve my low mood.

To sum up what I did: I carried out my daily affirmations, I did skin-to-skin with the twins, I drank plenty of water, I meditated and I went for short walks. Please do try any of these if you have the time to do so, because it may help you to feel so much better about yourself, physically, mentally, emotionally and socially. It will help to improve your health and wellbeing which is what you need after giving birth. Please also try some of these approaches with your husband or partner. It's a great way to spend some quality time together, to effectively communicate and too reconnect.

Survival tips for postnatal depression

Lauren from Colorado, USA.
Mother of triplets, two girls and one boy, aged two.
"I suffered from depression during my pregnancy when I was on bed rest for four months. I had a severely shortened cervix and had to have an emergent cerclage done. I didn't even realise I had depression so I didn't do anything about it, but after the children were born, I went on medication which I currently still take. I see a therapist which has made a huge positive difference. My PND started when my triplets were around one year old and it was very noticeable. I think that I was too overwhelmed to call it what it was up until that point. I still suffer from PND now and the triplets are almost three years old. I manage it the best I can. I mainly received support from my partner and through therapy.

If you have PND in your first year off parenthood, just remember you are not alone. This is so common; lots of women have experienced this. For me, medication helped me feel like myself for the first time in a long time. Once I was on medication, I realised how much of what I was feeling was related to the depression and not related to me personally. It is important you seek professional help so you can better cope."

Jaikisbell from Ohio, USA.
Mother of twins, one boy and one girl, aged eight months.
"I think my PND started the minute my kids were born. I felt guilty that they were born prematurely. Then, I was given the information that my daughter would probably die, I felt like I died myself. I made the decision to transfer my babies

to a different hospital in the hope that they would be able to help my daughter. She had a grade four intraventricular haemorrhage; in most babies it causes death. While at the hospital she was not doing any better and I kept blaming myself for it. I kept thinking that I should have followed the other doctor's opinion and just let her go, but she survived and could go home after 90 days of being in the NICU.

I honestly didn't cope with PND very well. I didn't think I had it, and instead I just spiralled out of control because of everything that was happening. I didn't have time to think about anything else. I ended up taking way too many sleeping pills, and that's when I hit rock bottom. I committed myself to a psych ward where I was institutionalised for three days. I spoke to different psychologists and psychiatrists and realised that asking for help was not a bad thing. I was then diagnosed with PND and given medication, which I took. I saw a psychologist for three months and was weaned off the medication.

Once my babies were home, I felt like a new woman, and I was the best mom I could be for them. As mothers we all go through struggles and speaking to someone can help, so don't suffer in silence. Speak to your doctor, your obstetrician or gynaecologist, a friend, and always ask for help! It takes a village to raise a child."

Lauren from Hull, UK.
Mother of twin girls aged four.
"I got postnatal depression three years after having the twins. It hit me like a ton of bricks. I still have anxiety now and I'm on medication for it. I'm not sure when it'll end. It's important not to be embarrassed or feel guilty. PND made me feel like I

was failing as a parent because the twins are developmentally behind. I didn't want to get up in the morning, I didn't want to wash, and the last thing I wanted was to be intimate with my partner. I shut myself away. It was my mum who noticed the early stages due to her suffering severely herself and she knew the warning signs."

Kristi from Southern California, USA.
Mother of triplets, two boys and one girl, aged two.
"I had postnatal depression for about three months after the babies were born. I brought the triplets home from the NICU at around two weeks old. During this time, I did a lot of crying, and finally spoke to my doctor, who provided help and advice and suggested taking antidepressant medication. It's important you get help as soon as you feel like you are suffering. There is no shame in asking for help, and taking medication to help you cope with the overwhelming responsibilities and life-altering changes that occur when you welcome multiples into your family. Reaching out to your doctor may be the safest place to start. They are there to help you, without judgement. You will likely feel isolated and overwhelmed, but it is important to manage your emotions and stability by seeking help.

At first I was embarrassed, and I didn't want to take medication. When I needed some help with the babies, I asked a neighbour and she offered to come over weekly to give me a small break. I never left the children completely in her care but would do laundry or dishes while she entertained the babies. She was great. She offered me adult conversation, hands-on assistance, and a much-needed breather. I cannot stress enough how helpful it felt to have her come for a few hours a week. She came for free, and she was heaven sent."

Cindy from South Africa.
Mother of twin girls aged one.
"I felt depression kicking in after birth as my twins were in the NICU for two weeks, and finally when they came home it was chaos. As a first-time mom I was really struggling with parenting both of them. I have to say I still have postnatal depression even to date; it's just that I am able to cope with it better. I have the support of my family and when things gets tough and I feel like I'm losing it I cry and pray for strength.

I am a midwife by profession therefore I would say it was easy for me to identify that I had postnatal depression and I am able to deal with it myself. However, I would advise a mother with PND that she must first accept that she has a problem, seek professional help or someone she can talk to and express how she feels. Find a good support system, and take some time out once in a while. Go for a spa treatment, a movie—just time for yourself. Please know it's okay to cry when you feel you're not coping."

Kristy from North Dakota, USA.
Mother of triplets, one girl, two boys aged two
"When I was 17 weeks pregnant, I underwent surgery due to having stage three twin to twin transfusion syndrome (TTTS) with my two boys, which is a rare complication of pregnancy that affects identical twins or other multiples sharing the same placenta and a network of blood vessels that supply oxygen and nutrients essential for development in the womb. This was

a very stressful time for me because from that day forward I was on bed rest and felt scared about losing them every day.

I believe my PND started three months after my triplets were born, when they came home from the neonatal intensive care unit. It lasted for about six months and was a very challenging time for me, as I experienced lack of sleep and lack of self-care. It was difficult to cope with PND whilst being a new mum of triplets, I talked to other parents who had TTTS and other parents who had triplets. I realised that I needed professional help so I spoke with a mental health doctor and psychiatrist who specialises in post-partum depression. I then realised I was also suffering from severe PTSD from my traumatic pregnancy. I was in complete survival mode!

I was given coping mechanisms such as breathing techniques to calm myself when triggered. I also spoke with my husband explaining what I was experiencing, which he didn't quite understand but he was supportive. I would advise any parent with PND and PTSD to seek help immediately and talk to anyone they feel comfortable enough to about how they feel. Everyone is different and may respond to traumatic events in a different way using different treatments to help manage trauma. It's also a good idea to find some support groups where you can openly speak with others who went through similar situations. Post-partum depression should not be ignored. I was in such a dark place."

Postnatal depression is as serious as conditions come and it can take over your whole life if not treated. As we can see from these tips provided, ensuring you have some help, support or treatment to manage the condition is extremely important, especially if you are breastfeeding. Some women with PND find it difficult to breastfeed or express milk when experiencing a world of emotions that they have no control over.

As I mentioned earlier, I experienced a very traumatic birth—which I think was one of the factors of my PND up until my twins were about seven months -I saw a doctor and was referred to counselling. But due to work commitments I didn't follow through straightaway. I did eventually attend one session but then I travelled abroad for a month which really helped me deal with how I felt. The change of scenery, hot weather and spending every day with my children without any distractions helped.

I think it's so important to have a strong support system as a parent. You need people around you to offer you support when you need it. If you don't have family and friends close by, speak to your doctor or health visitor who can provide you with advice and support groups. Also be aware of your temperament and character and how you deal with situations, and talk about how you feel; don't keep it in. Share your feelings with others so they can help you. Lastly, educate yourself about PND: do some reading, research, ask questions. There is help available to support you through this difficult and challenging time.

If you don't want to speak to someone face-to-face then you can go online and join some PND forums to see what other mums are going through; this might encourage you to open up because you'll realise you are far from alone in this.

If you can think of any other ways to help you deal with your postnatal depression please use the notes section below to jot down some ideas. And remember, whatever you do, finding time for yourself is the main focus here. You can include your partner, children, family and friends in some activities, but never forget the importance of self-care.

Let's not forget the fathers and partners who also experience postnatal depression. If that's you, take part in jotting down any ideas you have to support you and your partner through this overwhelming period in your lives.

My Notes

Jot down ideas for coping with postnatal depression and see what might help you

"If you don't ask, you don't get!"

-Stevie Wonder-

CHAPTER SEVEN

Don't Be Afraid to Ask

Here you are with your new expanded family. You have been blessed with multiple children; you are now home from the hospital ready to start your journey on the path of parenthood. You may feel scared, anxious and overwhelmed with all the things you have to do and you don't know where to start.

You have already organised your baby area with the essential items needed; you have rearranged your furniture to make your living arrangements more comfortable for you and your family. Therefore, all you need to focus on now is you and your newborns. Sounds simple, right?

Well, we all know that some of us don't have it as easy as that and may have other challenges to face. This chapter provides an insight into the importance of asking for help when you need it. Here I explain and provide information on the different types of help I asked for and received during the first year of parenthood. I am not one to shy away from asking for help, especially if I really need it, and honestly feel every parent should openly do the same if it makes their lives easier and less stressful. Raising one child has its challenges so if you are a parent of twins, triplets or more it's going to take more than a village—I'm sure you know how the sentence ends.

Being a new parent of multiples has its ups and its down and sometimes when we are experiencing the downs we might be in need of a little support. And yes, that's okay!. My motto is, if you don't ask, you don't get. There's no harm if the response is no—at least you tried, right?

I most definitely asked for help with my twins when I needed it and I wasn't afraid to ask for it. I honestly felt overwhelmed as a new mum and knew I was way out of my depth. For someone like me, who is quite meticulous and well organised, having children threw everything out of sync so I took all the help I could get. Luckily for Josh and I, we come from large families who are very supportive and helpful, so we had help from grandparents, siblings, friends and even our neighbour Tom who our children love dearly. We also had help from the twins' 10 godparents, yes 10! I know, we went overboard, but we felt this was needed considering there are two of them.

We received help and support as soon as we arrived home and this is where I must praise my mother who was there for us whenever we needed her; she knew exactly what to do and helped us organise everything we needed for the twins. She was our own personal Mother Theresa (her actual middle name is Theresa, which is quite fitting) and we are forever grateful for all she did for us.

I asked my mum to help with cleaning the twins' bottles, sterilising, washing clothes, ironing, cooking. The list continues. Whatever we needed, help with it was provided. We also had help and support from Josh's parents, Mary and Samuel (two more fitting names) who were naturals with the twins. When they came over I rested. I was relieved when they were there. I knew I could rest and not have to worry about anything. Josh and I felt very blessed to have such amazing grandparents in our lives especially because of all the different health problems I was experiencing.

As I said previously, I refused to suffer in silence with two dependent children, so as well as receiving help from grandparents we also received help from their godparents. We were lucky enough to have two of them that were available quite regularly to offer a helping hand.

My best friend Ayo visited often; she's really good with the girls, very calm and patient. Her presence alone made me feel more relaxed and less anxious and she often helped me with bath time. Just having some adult conversation made me feel normal again because I am a chatterbox and love conversing, and you don't get much of a response from two babies that aren't old enough to speak yet.

Another friend and lifesaver was Cassandra, who is like a big sister to me: humble, wise and gives the best advice. She's also very hands-on with the twins and I was able to go shopping or run errands whilst she looked after them. She also assisted with bath time and dinner time—a true diamond.

As often as the girls' godparents could come round, they would. It was always a pleasure to get visits from people who could help me with the twins. Sometimes I did think that I was asking for help too regularly but at the same time I didn't feel guilty for asking. I did what I had to do to survive.

I received a range of help from health and social care providers that support new parents and also assist you in your home. When speaking with my health visitor about how much I was struggling as a new mother with the twins, she informed me that there were a number of organisations that were available to offer me help, support and guidance. She even made referrals for me and I self-referred to some services as well. I took whatever help was out there. At this point I still didn't know I had postnatal depression but was experiencing a lot of the symptoms mentioned in Chapter six such as low mood, crying. severe anxiety, panic attacks, worrying that I wasn't a good mother, feelings of worthlessness, guilt and inadequacy—the list goes on. Below is a list of the various health and social care services I received support from.

Doctor (GP)

I must say my doctor was fantastic throughout the first year of us parenting. He was patient, caring and understanding. He also had previous experience working as a paediatrician. This made him knowledgeable on infants and common health issues they experienced under the age of one year old.

I often called my doctor's surgery to request a call-back from him regarding all the health concerns I was having with La Belle's feeding and diet, and my lack of sleep and not coping very well as a mother. I occasionally went into the clinic to see him if needed. In hindsight, I think I did call him a bit too often, but at the time I felt I needed to.

After speaking with my doctor and explaining all the different issues I was having he referred me to different health services which I was able to use. Some of them were community based and were able to visit me in my home which made life so much easier, less stressful and reduced my anxiousness.

Community Eczema Support for Infants

I received support from an eczema service provided through the NHS, who had a team of outreach eczema specialist nurses in my area that supported families with children of eczema. I had a wonderful nurse named Caroline who helped me with my daughter La Belle, who was allergic to milk and suffered from severe eczema, which meant I had to cover her hands in mittens to avoid her scratching herself until she would bleed. This service was especially helpful because the nurses were outreach, meaning they came to my home. I didn't have to worry or stress about having to get the girls dressed and take them out which was a nightmare for me in the beginning.

Every visit I had to complete a questionnaire relating to the severity of Bella's eczema; we discussed different creams and milks available for her skin type and her diet. What was really useful about this service was that the nurse had access to my daughter's medical records and was able to prescribe her medication to treat her eczema which saved me from having to book a doctor's appointment for this. In addition to this, the nurse provided food charts and different ways to monitor eczema flare-ups including how to treat them.

Health visitor

I am lucky to be blessed with a health visitor who is so accommodating, supportive, resourceful and empathetic. In the UK and other state-funded countries with health systems you'll find health visitors. These individuals are trained midwives or nurses that work in communities and people's homes to support families. A health visitor's role is to work with parents who have new babies, offering support and informed advice from the antenatal period until the child starts school at five years (www.babycentre.co.uk). They ensure young children have the best start in life with their growth and development, and that they meet their expected milestones.

When I first met my health visitor and found out she also has twin daughters of her own I honestly felt like I had been sent an angel from above. What are the odds that something like that happens? *Thank you Lord*, I said to myself.

Her daughters were a few years older than mine and during my twins' first year I was able to ask her all the questions under the sun about raising twin girls as well as gaining any help I could get whilst doing so. This really helped me understand certain things to do with being a twin mum, such as having a strong attachment to the girls, ensuring they had their vaccinations to protect them from diseases, how to change their nappies and ensure their private areas were cleaned properly as this process is different for boys. I also learnt what to expect as they got older, although she has always said to me that children grow differently, which is very true. Even though I have twins they have very different personalities and look very different. They also like playing with different toys and have different tastes in food.

My health visitor is very resourceful and has referred me to a number of health and social care organisations that have helped me with my twins, especially during the first year of their lives. I wish I could have her forever.

Twins Trust
I received help from the Twins and Multiple Births Association (TAMBA), now known as the Twins Trust, which can be found

online at www.twinstrust.org. My friend Claire who has twin boys recommended them to me and they gave me very useful advice for coping as a new parent of twins. What I really like about this organisation is that they are based all over the UK and offer parent meet-ups, playgroups and activities that you can participate in. One of their multiples playgroups was one of the first places I went to with the twins, where I met other parents and their twins and triplets.

They also offer help, information and advice online as well as over the phone. You also have the opportunity to take part in antenatal and parenting courses throughout the country which are very beneficial for parents who need to use these services.

Mother and baby clinic

Another service I was referred to was a local mother and baby clinic. In speaking with my health visitor she suggested it was a good idea to meet other mums whose circumstances were similar to mine. At first I was hesitant, but then thought it would be a good idea to get out of the house for some fresh air, a change of scenery and an opportunity to meet new people, which is something I love doing anyway.

So I attended the group and spoke with lots of mums; it was a welcoming and friendly place. I felt comfortable and relaxed in their presence. It was a great way to indulge in some adult conversation as well. The staff at the clinic were so helpful. I was able to speak to them one-to-one and they were able to refer me to other services available for mums. As I said previously, if you don't ask, you don't get, so I asked away. I was provided with so many outreach programmes, mother and baby groups and other clinics. I was spoilt for choice. I even managed to get a sleep therapist to come to my home and assist me with getting the twins into a good sleeping routine, which I struggled with as they kept waking each other up at night. Getting them both to sleep at the same time wasn't a problem. The issues occurred halfway through the night when one baby would wake up crying then disturb the other. I would end up with both girls awake at three or four am in the morning wanting to play. This went on throughout their first year so the sleep therapist came in handy.

In addition to this, there were also online support groups I found where I could interact with other mothers going through what I was. I received a lot of useful tips and advice on how to get the twins to sleep, pack a bag when taking them out, organise their clothes in drawers and cupboards, the right times to bathe them, cooking in bulk and freezing food for the whole family. These little things really helped me a lot halfway through their first year because it made me feel less apprehensive and insecure about what I was doing all the time and made me realise that I wasn't alone in how I felt.

Wow, I said to myself as I read different articles and blogs and participated in chat rooms for women going through all the things I had experienced. *I'm not crazy, I'm not alone, these things actually do happen to other mums.*

There were mums out there who had anxiety, who suffered from postnatal depression, who were sleep deprived, who struggled to bond with their children, who didn't want to leave their house because it was too much of a hassle. I could go on forever. Here are some of the online services/forums I used:

- www.twinstrust.org
- www.nhs.uk
- www.babycentre.co.uk
- www.bliss.org.uk
- www.kidshealth.org
- www.nhs.uk
- www.nct.org.uk

Also try:
- YouTube videos.
- Facebook—join a multiples group (there are loads).

I remember telling my husband about the different people I met online who were so helpful and supportive; they really put me at ease when I asked for help because they needed help too. I remember some mums saying they suffered in silence for months, not telling anyone what they were going through. They didn't want to be a burden or cause any hassle.

I was shocked by this because I thought every mum asked for help, but what I learnt was that some mums are private and they don't want to share their struggles with the outside world. Some mums never know where to start when seeking help until they join some mum forums online. Then there are mums who don't want to be a burden and mums like me, who ask anyone and everyone they can for a bit a help, support and guidance.

This is why I strongly believe in the power of communication. You don't need to leave your home if you don't feel comfortable doing so with your multiples. Give yourself time, and join in with some conversations online. You'll be surprised by the wonderful women you'll meet who share one thing in common:

We are all mothers.

And then there are the fathers or partners, who may need some help or support with being a parent to multiples. There are services available which are face-to-face or online. Just like I did, you can seek such information from your doctor or health visitor who can refer you to the different services available for you.

If you are working and don't have time available to attend groups or talk to someone face-to-face. Maybe you would just prefer to go online, there is also a lot of advice out there. Find something that relates to you and what you are going through.

To help you interact with other parents who might be able to help you I have listed some online services for you below. There are a variety of different things to read and there are some videos of dads talking about their experiences. I hope this helps and remember you are not alone on this journey. It's okay to ask for help if you feel you need it.

- www.thedadpad.co.uk
- www.dadsmatteruk.org
- www.isablog.co.uk
- www.parents.com
- www.healthyfamilies.beyondblue.org
- www.twinstrust.org
- www.my1styears.com
- www.webmd.com
- www.nct.org.uk
- www.twinsuk.co.uk

Also try:
- YouTube videos.
- Facebook—join a dads group or multiples group (there are loads).

Believe me when I say there are other mums and dads all over the world experiencing the same feelings you are. You might feel alone or isolated on this journey but I can tell you that you're not. I have connected with parents from Australia, America, Europe, Asia and Africa who have twins/multiple children and experience the same struggles, so please remember you are doing the best you can. And to let you into a little secret on the kind of help/support I asked for, here's my list:

- I asked family for help with housework (thank the Lord my mother enjoys ironing).
- I asked family for help with cooking.
- I asked friends to collect items from the shops for me, including my neighbour.
- I asked family and friends for help with shopping until I discovered online shopping.
- I asked my husband to help with the cleaning, but he said to hire a cleaner instead (no surprises there!).
- I got support with my anxiety and OCD through therapy.
- I got support with my hip problems by seeing a physiotherapist.
- I got support with the problems I was having with my left hand by seeing a hand therapist to treat de Quervain's tenosynovitis.

- I asked grandparents to watch the twins for a few hours whilst I slept.
- I asked my family and friends to watch twins if I needed to run some errands.

Survival tips for asking for help

Alan from Essex, UK.
Father of twin boys aged seven.
"I asked for help because parenthood can be quite challenging at times and the lack of sleep was very hard to deal with. I was lucky I had help from my mother and partner's mother who were both was very supportive. We also had help from close friends and other family members which was highly appreciated."

Kelly Ann from Essex, UK.
Mother of twin girls aged 11.
"Ask for help and take all the help that is offered to you because you will need it. If you are struggling don't try to do it on your own; there is help available—see you GP. Raising multiples is not easy and I was in a position where I had help and support with my children which I am truly grateful for. I received help and support from my mother who was a lifesaver and the Natural Childbirth Association (NCT) at www.nct.org.uk was helpful and supportive. They are the UK's largest parent charity and they provide practical and emotional support for mums during pregnancy and after."

Charlotte from London, UK.
Mother of triplets, two girls and one boy aged seven.
"Please don't be afraid to ask for help. I joined Facebook groups for parents with multiples; this was very helpful as there were thousands of mums from all over the world with multiples giving each other advice and tips which made all the difference.

I called on my friends and family as well, who were there for me when needed. It's good to have a strong network of people around you during this time. I also hired an au pair which was needed with triplets. Having someone there to help with the children made things less stressful which was exactly what was needed."

Jaikisbell from Ohio, USA.
Mother of twins, one boy and one girl aged eight months.
"I know some parents find in-laws a little irritating at times, but you hardly ever have to ask them for help; they are always glad to be there for you. Take their help! Remember: happy mommy = happy babies. It's useful to have your babies on a schedule, and do the same thing over and over and over. Babies learn patterns, and if you do the same thing every single time, they will eventually get there on their own!

My twins were not my first pregnancy. I was cocky and thought I knew better because I had done the mom thing before. WRONG! I did need help, and at first, I hated it, but then I realised that when I went to visit my in-laws, I would get three uninterrupted hours of sleep! Trust me, once you get a few minutes to take a shower, and take a good nap, you will never not ask for help!"

Lauren from Hull, UK.
Mother of twin girls aged four.
"I was never too scared to ask for help because I was too tired not to ask. I have a son who is five with special needs so always needed the help. We have a big family so someone was always there when I needed them to be which we really appreciated.

It also gave me some time to be me again and spend time with friends which was nice because there is not as much time for this during the first year of parenting."

Stephanie from Hertfordshire, UK.
Mother of twin boys aged two.
"Honestly, I'm not very good at asking for help, but what I would say is be open and honest about how you are feeling and if you need a break or are feeling overwhelmed tell your partner or anyone who could possibly help you so you can get some rest. Rest is so important and we don't get enough of it as mums! When I did ask for help it was because I was very tired, or I wasn't feeling very well, and this help mainly came from my husband.

All the help I received was useful and much appreciated. Just being able to go about my errands or supermarket shopping without twins was so much easier. You don't realise how easy it is to do chores before you have kids! Everything becomes a mission when you have twins. To make life a bit less stressful you could take one child shopping whilst the other remains with your partner/family I do this and its incredible how much easier it is!"

Now that you have read this, I sincerely hope you'll give yourself a break. All the different parents agree that help is needed, so please don't be afraid to ask for it. If you already have help or feel comfortable enough to ask for it then this is great because it can make such a difference in your first year as being a parent to multiples. We all want to survive this first year of parenthood the best way we can.

I hope my list above about the different types of help I asked for has given you some positive food for thought. Start thinking about who can help you and when; sometimes the help you may need cannot be planned in advance as you never know what to expect with children, so in this instance think about the people that you could ask for help last minute. This does tend to be parents, in-laws, siblings and close friends. Whoever you end up asking, just remember they are there to make life that little bit easier for you during this testing time.

What I'm about to say is important because I remember being given this advice by my friend Claire, who had twins a few years before me. I never listened to her until it was too late and I was completely exhausted. When you have family or friends come over to help and support you, let them do just that. Let them cook, let them clean, let them iron clothes, let them tidy up, just let them! I know you have your own way of doing things, just like I did, but during the first few months of parenting multiples let those around you support you by taking away any additional strain you might have. Let them be your saviour, let them be your knight in shining armour, let them be your support network—whatever you want to call them, just let them be there for you and your family.

I had so much support but I was trying to do all the housework, the cooking, the cleaning, organising baby clothes as well as looking after my twins until I couldn't take it anymore. My body was just too tired. When your body is so tired, just let it rest and recuperate. I should have just listened to Claire in the first place and embraced the help straightaway. And if I could go back and change things, that would definitely be one of them.

I have provided an area below for you and your partner to use when you need to ask for help. I have broken it down into three sections: family, friends and professionals such as your doctor or parenting group. All you need to do here is list the names of those that can help you and use this list as a useful reminder, especially in those moments of need. Be honest with yourself about who you can ask for help and remember you want people around you who will be supportive and helpful in meeting your needs.

Remember – it's okay to ask for help!

My Notes

List all of your family members who you can ask for help from

List all of your friends who you can ask for help from

My Notes

List all the support services you can receive professional help from

"Live with no excuses and travel with no regrets."

-Oscar Wilde-

CHAPTER EIGHT

Travelling with Multiples

I loved travelling abroad, especially to hot countries where I got to explore, sightsee, embrace the culture and indulge in their food. I loved the feeling of sand in my toes, the water from the clear blue sea around my ankles and lying on a deckchair, sunglasses on, reading a suspense novel that I just can't put down. Oh, how I loved those days.

Those sweet memories that are just that—memories. Yes, I say this in past tense because it's not something you can do with children under the age of one. Then again, why on earth would you want to travel with children abroad under that age? Sounds crazy, right? But I did it and yes it was stressful, but enjoyable at the same time, and that's what this chapter is about.

The aim here is to make your journey less stressful, more enjoyable and as easy as possible if you plan to travel abroad with your multiples under the age of one.

Before I get into the whole saga about me travelling aboard with multiples under the age of one, let me tell you what I experienced travelling abroad to Europe at just 16 weeks pregnant. I thought I would be fine because it was early on in my pregnancy and I was doing great for most part of the trip.

I decided to travel to Prague for a friend's birthday with some girlfriends for a long weekend. It was also my 37th birthday a few days after we were due to return so this was a little treat to myself as well. I felt quite positive about this trip. I had just finished my last counselling session, and I was managing my anxiety effectively so this trip was exactly what I needed. Some sun, culture and great food.

The day before I was due to fly to Prague I stayed the night in a hotel which was a few minutes away from the airport—I had an early morning flight. I remember arriving at the airport and checking in, and noticing a couple in the queue in front of me with a young baby in a car seat, I assumed only a few months old. I was thinking to myself, *I could never travel with my twins that young. I would be insane to do that; it would be hell on earth with all the different things I'd need to bring.*

We all boarded the plane fine. It was a pretty short flight, about one hour and 50 minutes. I managed to get some rest while on board and felt pretty relaxed, looking forward to my short break. Even though I was only 16 weeks pregnant I actually looked about five months pregnant, which I put down to carrying twins. However, I didn't even comprehend how big I could actually get and as I sat down in my allocated seat I remember thinking, *Thank God I can fit into my seat.*

When the plane landed my friend collected my things and we made our way to the exit; as I started walking down the stairs of the aircraft I felt the most excruciating pain in my pelvis area and nearly lost my balance. I had to quickly grab onto the railings for support. I had no idea what it was or where it came from and to be honest I was petrified. I actually had a panic attack because I thought I would have to go to hospital in Prague and didn't want to do so in another country. My friends were really concerned about me and I thought something was wrong with my babies.

"Please Lord, no, not now," I heard myself say.

After entering the airport and going through customs, we got a taxi to our hotel, and the pain had started to subside. I called my mother who works in a hospital and described the pain to her. She diagnosed it as Symphysis Pubis Dysfunction Syndrome (SPD) which is when your pelvic joints become stiff or move unevenly, and this can occur both at the front and back of your pelvis, causing a great deal of pain and discomfort when you move.

I researched this condition online and knew I had it instantly when looking at the different images, reading the different symptoms and watching a few YouTube videos. Doing the research and knowing what condition I had helped my anxiety decrease. I also remembered one of the tools for coping with anxiety which was to take big deep breathes to help you to relax. SPD is a very common condition in women which improves after childbirth. And luckily for me, especially at this point in time, the pain had eased somewhat and I was able to enjoy my short break in beautiful Prague. Even though I ended up walking around Prague like a constipated duck for the rest of my trip, I still had a really good time and did exactly what I'd planned to do—took in the sights, enjoyed the great weather, embraced a new culture, ate delicious food and shopped.

On my plane journey home I thought, *I'm not going to travel again throughout the rest of my pregnancy as this experience scared the shit out of me.* I had totally forgot that Josh and I had already booked our wedding anniversary holiday for that coming August. We were due to travel to four different European destinations over a two-week period.

I have previously seen plenty of pregnant women on aeroplanes and I'm sure there are many who feel safe enough to travel abroad whilst pregnant. In hindsight I should have spoken to my doctor before I travelled just to make sure everything was okay and whether there were any precautions to take before boarding a plane when pregnant.

Moving forward to August 2017, a couple of months after being back from my mini break in June. I unfortunately continued to suffer from SPD on and off throughout my pregnancy. I spoke to my husband about being scared to travel again whilst pregnant and he managed to reassure me. He believed I was just unlucky in Prague and told me to speak with my doctor before travelling on our anniversary holiday, which was exactly what I did.

I contacted my doctor a few weeks before we were due to fly to ask her if there was anything I needed to know or do during my pregnancy before travelling. There I was at the other end of the phone, with my notebook and pen in hand, ready to write down any important notes from our conversation that I needed to know, but instead, my page remained blank. My doctor told me I couldn't travel. I would be 27 weeks pregnant with twins and a number of health concerns. She didn't want me to experience any complications abroad, therefore travel at this point wasn't an option.

I was so upset and had to explain the bad news to my husband. I was thinking about all the money we had spent on our holidays so far to the different places we planned to go, but luckily enough when I called the travel companies we had booked with and informed them of my situation they were all able to give me full refunds. My doctor provided me with a doctor's note explaining why I couldn't travel so at least that was one less stress to worry about.

When the twins were around five months old I decided I needed a little sun for a few days before returning to work which was fast approaching. I spent some time thinking about where we should go for our first trip together as a family. We didn't want to travel too far away and wanted the flight to be as short as possible, but with nice beaches and family things to do whilst we were there. So, we looked at European countries not too far away from the UK and settled for Spain. Close to home, lovely beaches, inexpensive and lots to do.

The next step was getting the twins' passports. I cannot begin to describe how difficult it was to get a decent passport photo of the girls that met UK passport standards for babies, but I managed to succeed after going to get pictures taken on three separate occasions (they were either asleep, wouldn't wake up, fell asleep when we arrived, were crying or needed a nappy change). Anyway, we finally got the passports which arrived within a couple of weeks. I was so happy even though they both looked scared in their pictures along with mad-looking hair.

With finding somewhere to go in the bag, we started to research flights and accommodation. This took longer than expected because we were catering for four instead of two. Normally Josh and I would book our flight and hotel separately and travel to different places in and around Europe without a care in the world because it was so easy to do without kids.

However, I wasn't finding this easy at all. We spent hours upon hours looking for flights and accommodation that suited our needs and eventually managed to find both. At this point we felt good about ourselves. We had officially booked our first family holiday.

The next thing I did was research online how best to travel aboard with children under one year old. I came across some different parenting forums that provides reviews from parents who had done this in the past. To be honest, a lot of the reviews were overwhelming to read because I had a lot to think about such as the number of suitcases to take, car seats, the pushchair, baby clothes, toiletries, food and special milk and creams for my daughter La Belle who has allergies and eczema. Wow, it was a lot!

I got right down to it and started making a list of things I needed to pack, things I needed to buy and things I needed to get on prescription from my doctor. When I informed Caroline, the eczema nurse, about our family holiday she suggested I change La Belle's regular Hydromol skin cream, which is thick and oily, keeping her skin moist, especially in the winter, to something lighter. This was so she wouldn't burn in the sun.

Gosh! I felt like a bad mother when she suggested this because I hadn't thought about it at all. I had so much going on in my head I forgot something as important as this. My husband told me not to be too hard on myself, but I was, and I felt really guilty.

The doctor prescribed me a much lighter emollient cream called Zerobase, which is water based and wouldn't burn her in the sun. I also went to the pharmacy to get some sun protector for the twins, nearly forgetting I had to buy two different brands as the leading brand in the UK aggravated La Belle's eczema. I went to three different pharmacy shops and none of them could recommend me a sun cream that was gentle on eczema, they just recommended what was available to buy. I had to settle for a different brand that only had SPF 30 protection instead of SPF 50 which is recommended for children because their skin is more delicate and sensitive to burning.

Once all the packing was done and we arrived at the airport, I started to feel overwhelmed and anxious being surrounded by so many people in one space. I suppose I was feeling like this because it wasn't just Josh and I travelling; we had two little beings to care for and keep safe. When we checked in all our luggage we had to pay extra for it because we had a lot of things with us. We got to customs and yes, our bags were thoroughly searched by security, no surprises there! I was just glad we got to the airport earlier than normal just in case something like that happened.

I forgot to take out the baby milk which the security guard tried to throw away. I explained to him it was prescribed milk and showed him the prescription labels on the milk container. My other daughter Lourdes was on powdered SMA milk which wasn't a problem as I had the whole container with me unopened. When we finally got through customs, we went into Boots Pharmacy. I got speaking to a woman with her family who informed me that next time I travelled, I could pre-order baby milk in advance over the phone as prescriptions could be sent directly to Boots by my doctor. This way I could avoid issues with customs. I couldn't believe what I was hearing so asked the pharmacist in Boots who clarified this for me.

"Flipping brilliant," I said.

When boarding the plane, we could take the twins' pram all the way to the stairs of the plane which made life so much easier instead of having to carry it. Our plane journey lasted around two hours which went fast. The twins were sitting on our laps as children under two travel for free (but you still pay flight taxes); they were as good as gold and the plane staff were overly accommodating throughout. Our return journey went smoothly as we knew what to expect. The twins slept through the flight and we arrived back in the UK with no hitches.

So, you might have a rough idea of what you might need to pack in your suitcases when travelling with multiples. I have provided a list of things we packed for our first family holiday with the twins being six months old. These items went into our large suitcase:

- The first thing we did was buy a new, strong, sturdy luggage set which consisted of one large, one medium and one hand-luggage-size suitcase.
- Padlock for each suitcase.
- Baby carry-on car seats.
- Baby buggy and mosquito net to cover buggy.
- Baby slings.
- Plug converters.
- Phone charges.
- Small portable fan.
- Insect repellent suitable for babies.
- Sun protection (www.sunsense.co.uk).
- Baby blankets.
- Towels, flannels.
- Baby play mat and a bag of light toys.

- Clothes, shoes, swimwear, bibs, muslins, sun hats.
- Baby food and dry snacks.
- Baby plastic spoons.
- Dummies and dummy clips.
- Large pack of nappies (bought more once we arrived).
- Sensitive baby wipes x6.
- Dove baby wash for Lourdes.
- Oilatum baby wash for La Belle.
- Palmer's cocoa butter lotion for Lourdes.
- Prescribed Zerobase emollient cream for La Belle.
- Powdered SMA milk for Lourdes.
- Prescribed powdered milk for La Belle.
- Bottles.
- Microwave sterilising bags and sterilising tablets.
- Other toiletries including hair oil, hydrocortisone cream.
- Hair brush.
- Children's first aid kit (purchased from John Lewis).
- Baby thermometer.
- Hand sanitiser/gel (plenty of them).
- Surface wipes.

Here's a list of what I packed in the twins' carry-on bag so that my husband and I had easy access to them in the airport and on the plane:

- Sets of change of clothes (4 sets for twins) x2.
- Blankets x2.
- Bibs, muslins.
- Hand wipes and gel.

- Dummies and dummy clips.
- Soft toy each.
- Sophie the Giraffe teether each (lifesavers).
- Plastic toy keys each.
- Bottles x4.
- Handful of nappies (based this on having twins and length of flight).
- Small nappy cream.
- Nappy sacks.
- Sensitive baby wipes x2.
- Foldable changing mat.
- Powder milk divider.
- Baby snacks.
- Small bottled water.

Our second family holiday was when the twins were 13 months old. We went to Mexico for Christmas and New Year which was lovely. We were much more organised the second time round with what to buy in advance and what to pack, and our twins were eating solids so we didn't have to worry too much about packing certain food and milk.

I finally managed to find a suitable sun protector for my daughter La Belle after having a conversation at her hospital appointment with a renowned allergy specialist in London, Dr Fox. I explained I would be travelling at the end of the year and asked whether he knew of any sun protection cream for children with eczema. He recommend Sunsense SFP 50+ which I managed to find in a large Boots pharmacy. I packed this to take with us and it worked perfectly. La Belle's skin was fine and she didn't scratch at it throughout the trip. I could even use it on both girls, myself and my husband. It's the best brand I've ever used for sun protection and I highly recommend it. As an eczema sufferer myself this worked wonders for me. I wish I had discovered this brand sooner.

In addition to Sunsense I also packed some aloe vera gel (www.optimah.com) and Childs Farm lotion (www.childsfarm. com) for La Belle. I briefly mentioned I used these products on her in Chapter five, which I purchased from our local health foods store. These products are really useful in treating eczema.

As I also mentioned in Chapter five, Josh and I wanted to use more natural products on La Belle's skin and avoid using the prescribed steroid creams and ointments. There are quite a few brands of aloe vera gel but we have stuck to Aloe Pura. We use it more so in the summer or when the weather is warm as a type of cooling cream for Bella when her skin flares up; it reduces skin redness and irritation just like the Childs Farm products do. We use the bath wash and un-fragranced lotion all year round. This is also used on Lourdes and helps keep the twins' skin moisturised and hydrated. I highly recommend these products. They are brilliant for kids and have been fully dermatologically tested.

Once everything was packed we decided to drive to the airport and leave our car there. We took our slimline double buggy with us only, weighing 10kg, which was perfect to use whilst abroad. I searched high and low for a suitable twin buggy that was light in weight and light in price. Hey presto! I found one. This time round, there were no issues with suitcase weight, no issues going through customs. It was plain sailing for us as our first holiday fully prepared us for the second. I even remembered to pre-order La Belle's special milk which I collected at the chemist in the airport. Once again, we were able to take the twins in their buggy all the way to stairs of the plane and board safely.

The only thing that was awful about this trip was the plane journey there and back – absolutely awful. Having the children sit on our laps for over 10 hours each way was a complete nightmare as the girls wouldn't keep still when they were awake, and the seating space was small. I had to keep moving in and out of the seat to stretch my legs and entertain the twins. Unfortunately all the extra leg room seats were already taken. In addition to this, one thing we didn't realise and wasn't told when we booked our all-inclusive packaged holiday was that even though we paid taxes for the twins' flights because they sat on our laps they were not entitled to a meal on the plane. I was furious as it was the first time we had booked a package holiday. The plane staff once again were very accommodating and did provide food for the girls which I was very grateful for. Luckily enough I had lots of snacks with me, but my advice to you before booking any package holiday with children under two that don't have a seat is to do all the research you need to about your holiday and ask all the questions that come to mind so you know what to expect on your holiday. Every airline has their own rules.

Here is a list of things we packed in our large suitcase for our second holiday. Bear in mind that the twins were a little older:

- Padlock for each suitcase.
- Baby buggy and mosquito net to cover buggy.
- Plug converters.
- Phone chargers.

- Small portable fan.
- Insect repellent suitable for babies.
- Baby blankets.
- Towels, flannels.
- Baby play mat and a bag of light toys.
- Clothes, shoes, swimwear, bibs, muslins, sun hats.
- Dry snacks.
- Range of different cereals.
- Baby plastic spoons.
- Dummies and dummy clips.
- Large pack of nappies (bought more once we arrived) x2.
- Sensitive baby wipes x2.
- Childs Farm baby wash and lotion for twins.
- Aloe vera gel for La Belle.
- Prescribed powdered milk for La Belle.
- Bottles/beakers.
- Microwave sterilising bags and sterilising tablets.
- Other toiletries including hair oil.
- Hair brush.
- Children's first aid kit (purchased from John Lewis).
- Baby thermometer.
- Hand sanitiser/gel (plenty of them).
- Surface wipes.

Here's a list of what I packed in the twins' carry-on bag so that my husband and I had easy access to them in the airport and on the plane:

- Change of clothes x3.
- Blankets x2.

- Bibs, muslins.
- Hand wipes and gel.
- Dummies and dummy clips.
- Toy mobile phone each.
- Cuddly bear each.
- Sophie the Giraffe teether each.
- Small pack of nappies (based this on having twins and length of flight).
- Small nappy cream.
- Nappy sacks.
- Sensitive baby wipes x2.
- Foldable changing mat.
- Powder milk divider.
- Baby snacks.
- Bottle each, beaker each.
- Small bottled water.

Here are some useful websites with information and advice about travelling with multiples abroad:

- www.whattoexpect.com
- www.nhs.uk
- www.babycentre.co.uk
- www.emmasdiary.co.uk
- www.babycantravel.com

Survival tips for travelling abroad with multiples

Kris from California, USA.
Mother of triplets, two boys and one girl aged two.
"Road trip! We first travelled by car with the triplets from California to Phoenix when they were just two months old. This was a long road trip which took nine hours by car. We regularly stopped for breaks to feed the children and do diaper changes. And we had my mom and dad come with us, including their cat and dog, who were all in the car behind us. We stayed in Phoenix for two months because we have a house there then returned home to California.

We then travelled again when the triplets were seven months old, but this time by plane. We flew from California to Canada which takes roughly five hours. I must say the kids were fine on the plane which made life so much easier. We ensured they had their teethers, a toy to play with and plenty of snacks. We then flew from Canada to Phoenix, another five-hour flight, and stayed there for 10 days then flew back home to California.

If you are planning to travel with your multiples under the age of two remember it is free to do. With regards to packing for a holiday it's best you make a list and tick things off as they go into the suitcases. I didn't spend a long time deciding which triplet would wear what, I just packed clothes; it made things easier for me.

Make sure you and your partner have a carry-on bag for the plane with all the essentials needed. With triplets you'll need two bags. I packed my breast pump, breast milk in bottles ready to drink as well as formula milk which I just added hot water to. Once you have packed, I would make another checklist of the things you need to take when leaving the house to go to the airport; this is so you don't forget anything. It's important you pack sensibly and be realistic with the things you need. As well as luggage you have your children and pram as well. I must admit we found it much easier to travel with our kids under the age of one because when they started walking, they just wouldn't keep still on our travels."

Josh from London, UK.
Father of twin girls aged two.
"When we travelled to Spain with our daughters, they were seven months old. We had a great time. We'd decided we didn't want to go too far from the UK for our first trip so Spain was ideal.

One thing I noticed was there were so many things my wife packed for the twins! I was wondering where it was all going to go, but she managed to find a place for every item we took. She had a list prepared in advance which was needed and I would recommend this to other parents just so you don't forget anything you need, especially if any of your multiples have prescriptions from your doctor."

Shelby from Pennsylvania, USA.
Mother of triplets, two girls and one boy aged nine months.
"We travelled from Pennsylvania to Arizona with our triplets which was a five-hour flight. They were six months old and luckily, we didn't experience any real complications. We planned around the twins' sleeping time so when we were going there, we took a flight that started at their bedtime. They slept the entire way. On the way home was a morning flight, and it was harder keeping them entertained. We fed them during take-off

and landing and fed on-demand during the flight (we have scheduled feeds normally). My husband and I travelled with my two brothers. The airline policy was one baby per lap (we didn't pay for extra flight seats), so we needed three adults, then my other brother came to help carry luggage which made all the difference. I was very grateful for family.

If you plan to travel with your multiples under one year old, it's a good idea to arrange for an order pick-up at your destination. Order everything from diapers, wipes, formula, to medicine and gas drops. If you have a lot of extras left over at the end of your trip, you can donate or pack it to take home. While on the plane, bring a bag of toys and snacks for each baby. Anything that you would need to take out for inspection in security, have prepared in a separate backpack. It was much easier to hand the agent one bag for inspection rather than pulling items out from various bags. We kept the babies in their triple stroller for travel through the airport with a ring of toys attached at each seat to keep them occupied."

Stephanie from Hertfordshire, UK.
Mother of twin boys aged two.
"We travelled to Germany with our twins under the age of one and the first thing I did was write a list of the different things that needed to be packed, which I ticked off as I went along. This is a really good way to monitor what you are taking on holiday and avoid overpacking. I would also suggest you spread various items across suitcases in case bags get lost and you don't want to be left without baby essentials. If you can, use separate travel pushchairs, as they are good for hanging bags on and it is much easier to get babies through an airport in a

pushchair instead of holding them along with hand luggage. If you have newborn babies you could put them in a sling to make travelling easier for you. What's also great about using a pushchair is that you can take it all the way to the aircraft walkway before boarding the plane and it's there for you at the other end to continue your travels.

If you have an iPad or tablet pack it in your hand luggage; this was a lifesaver for us on the plane. Have a lot of snacks for babies if they are on solid foods. Ensure you also have a lot of baby wipes at your disposal as you will need them throughout plane journey."

April from Utah, USA.
Mother of quadruplets, one girl and three boys aged four.
"My husband is in the U.S. Air Force and when I was pregnant we were stationed in Alabama, therefore we had no family around, no extra help, which was hard, but we worked well as a team. When our quads turned eight months we moved to Utah. Travelling by plane from one state to another was an unforgettable journey with our quads and other three children. We are a family of nine!

When packing for travelling abroad with multiples it's important to have a list of the things you need to take. Since I have quadruplets I made each one a separate, large, zip-lock bag with their name on it for all their snacks/food, books and favourite small toys/animals. Anything that my quads share I put together in a larger bag. I always pack additional items such as extra outfits, nappies, wipes, pacifiers, bottles, medication, Sippy cups and bibs. In addition, I'll pack a phone charger, computer, iPad headphones, baby clothes, shoes, socks, jackets and any other essential items for the plane journey.

Travelling with multiples via plane doesn't have to be a nightmare. It's important you plan your journey to avoid any stress or hassle once on the plane. Be sure to take your car seats, strollers, infant chest carriers and anything else that will still help you have free hands to deal with plane tickets and security lines, and just try to stay positive and know it can be done. Don't worry what people are thinking around you when going through customs; you might take longer than the average person because you have more children and items with you to be searched. Don't feel pressured.

When boarding the plane, as I walk down the aisle I usually say something to the passengers sitting around me such as, "I hope you all brought ear plugs, or they're usually pretty good when we travel, but I'll apologise now just in case they decide to give us a run for our money this time." This is just to break the ice in case all goes wrong. Ha ha! We have met some wonderful and kind people when we travel that it can really make for a great experience. I also like to try to plan nap times or feeding times around when we're in the air; it tends to keep the quads a bit calmer. If you have babies that are still breast or bottle feeding, or have dummies, it will tremendously help if you feed them during take-off and landing, so that their little ears can pop properly and help them be comfortable and relaxed."

Wow, I take my hat off to anyone who travels abroad with multiples. No matter how much you plan and prepare for your journey you can never predict what might happen. We all hope any plane journey leaving from the front doors of our homes all the way to our destination goes smoothly especially with little multiples in tow.

When you book a flight or package holiday with multiples under the age of two they can travel for free (you just pay taxes) but they have to sit on an adult's lap (one child per adult). But you cannot sit next to each other on the plane as one party. When my husband and I travelled to Spain with the twins he sat in the row behind me which was inconvenient as we had to keep swapping the twins over as they were getting irritable having to stay in one place for so long. There is a safety reason for this which is the number of air masks available per person in case of an emergency.

What was interesting is the plane staff were fully knowledgeable on this information but the airport staff and travel agency I booked with weren't. I thought this might be due to who we were flying with but no, the same thing happened when I booked a family holiday to Mexico. The travel agent I booked with wasn't aware—they had to call the airline for clarification—but the plane crew once again were aware.

It's advisable you book your seats in advance, just like Kris from California said she did, that way you're comfortable with where you're sitting. Extra leg room seats are useful especially with children under two years old who have to sit on your lap unless you pay full price for them to have their own seat. If your children are under one year of age and under 30lbs you can book baby bassinets for any flights that are long-haul. They are pretty handy and come with bedding and sheets. They hook directly onto the bulkhead in front of your seat. Reserving these items is very important due to them being limited and you need to make sure that you reserve them for both outbound and inbound flights as soon as you book your holiday. If this is something that you think your family would benefit from, contact the airline directly before paying for your flight or package holiday.

If you are planning a holiday or short break away with your family, I have provided you with two checklists to help you plan what to pack. The first checklist is for your hand luggage/carry-on bag and the second checklist is for what to pack in your suitcases. When completing your checklists I would advise you to research where you are going because if they have local amenities you can then pack lighter. For example, if you can purchase nappies, sun protection and baby wipes abroad this will save you having to pack these items in your suitcase. Taking fewer bags when travelling amounts to reduced stress levels.

Travelling checklist

What to pack in hand luggage

Travelling checklist

What to pack in suitcases

"May it be light to you in dark places, when all other lights go out."

-J.R.R. Tolkien-

CHAPTER NINE

Light at the End of the Tunnel

Can you see it? That bright shining light in front of you? That's the light at the end of the tunnel letting you know that everything is going to be just fine. Things will get better, and you are doing a fantastic job raising your children. Yes, it's challenging, exhausting, physically draining, and a complete nightmare at times, but just hold on a little longer. That light of hope and change is fast approaching; it's closer than you think.

This chapter focuses on the bright lights, which in actual fact are those moments in your first year of parenting multiples when things start to get that little bit easier.

The metaphoric expression 'there's light at the end of the tunnel' dates back to the 1800s, but became widespread only in the mid-1900s. It always makes me think that there is a solution to a difficult situation—the solution being that ever so bright light you are waiting for, that sign things will change for the better.

When my twins were a few months old all I wanted to do was hide somewhere and sleep forever. It felt like I hadn't slept in years. I no longer had that radiant appearance whilst being pregnant. You know that look I'm talking about? When people comment and say, "You look great! You're glowing." I hadn't heard that in a long while.

At this point in my life I was far from glowing. My hair wasn't combed and the thought of washing it was non-existent. I was constantly covered in sick and baby drool, surrounded by nappies, cotton wool, baby powder and cream. My skin felt dry and I looked ashen, I was living in baggy night shirts and flip-flops. I kept asking myself, "When will things get better? How long does it take? Where is that bloody light at the end of the tunnel?"

All I could see was complete darkness, not even a flicker to give me some sort of comfort or hope that things would get easier. It was like being a solider in the trenches trying to find a way out. However, my saving grace came in the form of angels: my wonderful family and friends who had already had children and experienced what I was feeling understood what I was going through.

They often encouraged me to keep my spirits up, provided me with comforting words of wisdom, and gave me a hug when I needed it. As I felt really low and depressed, they would reassure me things would change for the better and I should to try to remain positive which is difficult to do when all you can smell is breast milk and poop. However, they did support me with housework, cooking, cleaning and ironing, but most importantly they would tell me their stories of motherhood in the first few months, their struggles and challenges and then finally about seeing that bright light at the end of the tunnel as their children started to approach a year old.

Hearing this made a world of difference for me, so much so it provided me with some relief. I would always think negatively about certain aspects of parenting such as not feeding and burping them right, not putting them to sleep in the correct position, bathing them incorrectly. This had a lot to do with my anxiety and thinking that I wouldn't be a good enough parent to my children and I would constantly make mistakes and get things wrong. So, whenever I heard positive stories from family and friends about their children, it left me feeling hopeful.

Reflecting on my pregnancy as a mum of twins, I experienced plenty of highs and lows (more lows unfortunately) throughout my 37 weeks and four days of carrying them and the different trimesters I went through. Come to think of it, not once did I research or ask my doctor or midwives what was expected to happen during these different stages of pregnancy. I did not prepare myself for this part of my pregnancy and in hindsight genuinely wish I had because I know it would have massively contributed to a reduction in the levels of anxiety I was battling with.

I knew that women went through three trimesters in their pregnancy, but what I didn't know was the different effects these trimesters had on the body. Normally I am the kind of person who is on the ball, head screwed on, always carrying a diary and very organised, especially when it comes to such important matters as this, but clearly this was something I completely forgot about during this busy period of my life. It went completely over my head.

The funny thing is that I researched trimesters after the twins' first birthday. I'm not sure what made me want to do this but I'm so glad I did because it answered a lot of unexplained questions I had in my pregnancy regarding how I felt, physical changes and the different times some unexplained things happened, such as leg cramps and heartburn.

I repeatedly asked myself when on earth would I would see the light at the end of the tunnel? As well as me asking myself this plenty of times during my first year as a mother, it happened a lot during the 37 weeks and four days.

Let's talk about trimesters because I'm sure every mum looks forward to getting through each stage as easily and safely as possible. There are three trimesters in a pregnancy and they are broken down into weeks. During the three different trimesters you are expected to experience different symptoms and you will see your body change.

The following chart shows each stage of pregnancy and the symptoms you may experience during each stage. Not all women will have every symptom mentioned here as every pregnancy is different.

Trimester	Month	Week	Symptoms
1	1	1-4	Backache, heartburn, constipation, breast tenderness, morning sickness, feeling tired, weight gain, indigestion, bloating, skin becomes oily, hair and nails grow rapidly.
	2	5-8	
	3	9-12	
2	4	13-17	Skin and muscles stretch, constipation, more weight gain, increased appetite, headaches, increased backache, leg cramps, gestational diabetes may occur.
	5	18-22	
	6	23-28	
3	7	29-31	More weight gain and backache, rib pain, heartburn, stretch marks, change in balance and mobility as your stomach grows, anxiousness, haemorrhoids, feeling heavy, shortness of breath, pain in bum and pelvis, swelling in ankles, fingers and face, trouble sleeping, contractions.
	8	32-35	
	9	36-40	

Based on this chart I would say I experienced most of the symptoms especially the heartburn which was constant throughout the second and third trimesters. The level of anxiety

I had before and during pregnancy grew in size as I did. The sleeping or lack of it was awful. I experienced problems with this in the second and third trimesters.

Due to being pregnant during the summer I felt like I was overheating. I literally had two buns in the oven on full heat mode. I constantly had my fan on during the day and at night to try to keep cool. The worst of it was I couldn't sleep lying down because I was so hot and also in pain. I couldn't lie on my left or right sides for too long due to the shooting pains and cramp I experienced in my side and legs. I was advised by my midwife not to lie on my back in order to prevent blood clots and for obvious reasons I could not lie on my stomach. This was hell on earth for me. Some nights I slept upright, outside my front door where it was cool, on the pouf my husband purchased for me to elevate my feet. I would lean on the wall for support and just sleep. My husband tried his best to support me but that was the only way I could rest comfortably. At this point giving birth was something I wanted to happen soon.

Now, when I said I couldn't wait to see the light at the end of the tunnel, I meant it with all my heart, body and soul, and as I was wheeled into the delivery room to give birth, that light was electrifyingly bright.

Whether you are in the first few months of your pregnancy or parenting, when reading this I highly recommend you talk to family and friends who have already had children to know what that bright light looks like. Empathy goes a long way during pre and postnatal pregnancy.

I remember my husband saying when the twins were born all they would do in the first few months as newborns was sleep. He thought they wouldn't cry or need constant attention, they'd just want milk and sleep. I kept telling him that he was delusional, and he should talk to some of his friends about their experiences as new fathers, but he said he was fine and he was prepared. However, when the twins arrived and we came home from the hospital, he didn't understand why they wouldn't just sleep and soon realised what he'd said was insane! He never got any sleep and was constantly feeding and changing them. He looked tired and withdrawn. It's incredible what physical changes we experience with our bodies when we are stressed and sleep deprived.

I remember him asking me once, "When will it get easier?"

I felt sorry for him. He was working long hours and being a new parent of twins was taking its toll. It was very visible. I could tell he was in desperate need of seeing some light at this point in our parenting journey.

By the time our twins started holding their own bottle and my husband and I no longer had to tandem feed, the light at the end of the tunnel started to come through. When they could sit up on their own, the light at the end of the tunnel became brighter. When they started eating solids, my oh my, that light became blinding. By them just doing these little things our lives as parents became much easier.

I wasn't carrying them as often as I used to and this really helped my left wrist as I suffer from de Quervain's syndrome, which is inflammation of the tendons in your wrist and lower thumb, caused by a number of issues, one being hormonal changes in pregnancy, so the less carrying I did the better it was for me (www.familydoctor.org).

In my first year of parenting I had two courses of corticosteroid injections to help treat de Quervain's syndrome due to the pain I experienced in my wrist. It was unbearable. This involved a long needle being inserted into the joint in my wrist to help reduce the inflammation around my wrist and thumb. There was a point when the twins were around three to four months old when I couldn't lift them up with my left hand due to this condition. My husband had to pick the twins up for me and rest each one in my arms, which was difficult at times.

I struggled with certain things at home when I was alone. For example, I couldn't use my left hand to open a door. If I bent the door handle down the sharp pain that I would feel right along my thumb and wrist was indescribable. I couldn't open a jar of food. I couldn't use both hands to do up buttons on a shirt or coat or use my left wrist to push myself up when getting out of the bath. It was a nightmare. I had to wear a brace and still wear one now. So I have to be very careful with what I lift or move to avoid aggravating the joint.

That light at the end of the tunnel also became bright for us when the twins learnt how to crawl and then walk. Lourdes learnt how to crawl and walk before La Belle. They were both walking before their first birthday and as I watched them develop during their first year I noticed even more so how they were developing at different paces. Sometimes people assume because you have multiples their stages of developmental milestones are the same but they couldn't be more wrong.

Out of all the special moments I witnessed, the twins starting to walk on their own was the most precious moment for me. Watching the girls take their first steps was even more special because I didn't miss the moment; I managed to see them both do this for the first time. My husband said his most precious moment was when his daughters first opened their eyes and just stared at him, then smiled at him after hearing the sound of his voice.

The twins starting to walk really helped ease the pressure and strain I had in the right side of my hip. Whilst pregnant my hip moved out of place due to my stomach being heavy from carrying my twins. This was very painful and uncomfortable especially when walking and trying to sleep. Josh purchased me a pregnancy girdle to help ease the pressure off somewhat and it really helped with the pain I was experiencing. It improved a great deal and I continued to wear it occasionally after I gave birth because of my hip still causing me some discomfort.

Things really do start to get easier as your children get older and yes there are new challenges, but they can be taken on more positively when you have had more sleep. You start to feel human again and feelings of complete despair fade away. You become more experienced in the field of parenting and your confidence levels do start to increase, so hang on in there, your light is coming.

Here are some examples of when parents first started seeing that light at the end of the tunnel within the first year of parenthood:

- When your children first smile at you.
- When you are finally able to get a good night's sleep.
- When you can wash your hair, have a long shower or relaxing bath without being disturbed.
- When your children start to walk.
- When your children can hold their own bottle and you no longer have to tandem feed.

There are so many precious moments that children go through in their first year of development that you want to capture, and as parents we always want to bear witness to such treasured moments so that we can cherish them forever.

So that you remember when these special moments occur, on the following pages I have provided you with a chart to list all the special things your children do within their first 12 months. This way you'll have these memories forever and when your children get older you can tell them when they first began to lift their heads, babble, laugh and giggle, sit up unsupported, start crawling, and even when they said their first words.

Your children's special moments of development

Month	Child's name	Special moment	Date/Time

Your children's special moments of development

Month	Child's name	Special moment	Date/Time

Your children's special moments of development

Month	Child's name	Special moment	Date/Time

Survival tips for finding light at the end of the tunnel

Lesley from Scotland, UK.
Mother of triplet girls aged two.

"That light became bright for us when we discovered little handles for the triplets' bottles and they could hold them themselves! They stopped needing to be fed through the night and they learnt to self-settle at night as well as nap during the day. When they moved into their own room and were old enough that we turned the volume on the baby monitor down to silent so we didn't let every little whimper disrupt our sleep. They started interacting with each other and playing together. When they told me they loved me it makes me instantly forget all the hard times in those first few years (and almost want to do it all over again... maybe not!)."

Kelly Ann from Essex, UK.
Mother of twin girls aged 11.

"Every day, week and month presents new challenges. There are more successes and more failures but I have loved every moment of it. Nobody's perfect no matter what they show the world on social media. Just do your best. I realised there was light at the other end of tunnel every time I saw a smile or heard a giggle which made me feel very proud. I could see they were developing into two very happy little girls."

Josh from London, UK.
Father of twin girls aged two.

"I started to see light at the end of the tunnel when my twins started walking and talking. Carrying them everywhere reduced and I didn't have to constantly worry about them falling over. Enjoy the process and try to look at things from your children's perspective not yours. As a father I learnt how different my daughters' personalities are. I had it in my head that because they were twins a lot of things would be the same—how mistaken I was! But I learnt as they got older to understand their needs and wants which made life so much easier for me."

Ebony from London, UK.
Mother of twin girls aged nine.
"I started to realise there was light at the other end of tunnel when my girls started walking. It was nice to see them starting to become more independent. They made me very happy. You may have those moments where things start to get a bit too much and it's all just too stressful, but as they get older it does gets easier. Enjoy the journey as it goes very quickly and before you know it's they're already in primary school. During this first year try to take loads of pictures so you can look back at how well you've done as a parent."

Paul-Michael from London, UK.
Father of twin girls aged three.
"When our twins started to communicate more with each other and acknowledge one another's presence this was nice to observe. My daughter Eva, the older twin, first said, "I love you" at only a few months old. She sounded out the words one day out of the blue whilst being changed. It's something I say to the twins daily. This made me smile.

Also watching them grow and become more independent made me a very proud and happy father. I could see progress was being made. If you ever feel like you are struggling, please remember that it does get much better as they grow. If you are not sure about how to do something for your children, never hesitate to ask your partner or the support structure around you. As you get to learn about your children's likes and dislikes, personality and character traits, the light in the tunnel becomes even brighter."

Carmen-Angela from Rostock, Germany.
Mother of triplet girls aged one.
"The first time I started to see light at the end of the tunnel was when our triplets started to only wake up once throughout the night. It was magical that we could sleep more; we were so happy when this started to happen. The sleep deprivation was so difficult, and we were woken up throughout the night so many times it was so hard to get a good night's sleep. Just after the age of one our triplets started to hold their own bottle which was great for us as feeding three children at the same time had its challenges. We could see they were becoming more independent which was fantastic to observe."

It's so nice to be part of your children's development, to watch them grow, learn new skills, explore through play and then eventually start walking and talking. I'm sure all parents embrace the different types of development with open arms. I truly believe it's the little steps of progress they make that are the most treasurable, just like Ebony said. When her twins started walking that's when she could see light at the end of the tunnel. I felt exactly the same with my twins; them walking and becoming more independent was heaven on earth for me.

I was so happy, twice over, when this happened which helped my anxiety levels to decrease considerably.

All parents will have their own stories of when they started to see light at the end of tunnel and these stories will be unique to them because all children are different and have their own personal experiences as they grow. If you are nearing the one-year-old milestone or haven't yet reached it believe me when I say it's a wonderful feeling and it should be celebrated, not just because it's your children's birthday but because it's your day too. Celebrate how far you have come and what you have achieved, which I talk about in more detail in the next chapter. And please remember you are doing an amazing job raising multiples, which we all know isn't easy, so when we experience those bright-light moments we need to hold on to them dearly and give thanks to our accomplishments.

"I had no idea that history was being made, I was just tired of giving up."

-Rosa Parks-

CHAPTER TEN

You Survived!

Yaaay you survived! Your children are one year old!

You made it! You did it! You achieved it!

Welcome to the club of things will start to get easier!

Give yourself a round of applause. Dance out your happiness. Sing it from the rooftops. "Yesssss, I survived the first year of parenthood!"

If you are reading this chapter, then a huge congratulations to you. It may have been a whirlwind of emotions, trials and tribulations, but you have got to the other end in one piece. Your children are 365 days older and you are 365 days wiser, stronger, more experienced, knowledgeable, grateful and of course thankful.

Stop!

Take a minute!

Just think about your journey and how far you've come.

For some it will have been a bit easier than expected to reach this milestone, but for others, like myself, it was a real challenge and a struggle. Regardless, you are here so embrace it, celebrate it and enjoy it because all you have to do now is watch your children grow into the independent beings they'll become, with a little help from you of course, but it will get easier.

When our twins turned one, my husband and I gave each other a high five. We celebrated La Belle and Lourdes' birthday with a party which all our close friends and family attended. It was such an amazing celebration and an emotional one too. I had to thank everyone who had helped raise our children over the last year, who supported us at home with the cooking, cleaning, ironing, babysitting. Josh and I were overly grateful and thankful. It was lovely to spend time with all our family and friends under one roof for the first time since the twins arrived. I was overwhelmed with all the admiration I received.

- "Congratulations!"
- "Well done."
- "You've done an amazing job."
- "You raised beautiful girls."
- "You're blessed."
- "Fantastic parents."
- And of course, "You survived the first year!"

Hearing comments like these made me smile and cry at the same time, but my tears were tears of joy. My friends and family often tell me I make parenthood look easy, that I handle it very well, which I think is bizarre because any parent full well knows it isn't. But what's even more crazy is when I hear this from complete strangers and think to myself, *they are completely bonkers*.

Even though I've had plenty of joyous moments with the

girls that ultimately outweighed all the stress, anxiety and lack of sleep I experienced it was still an overwhelming, challenging first year that I don't think I'll ever forget.

I remember just before our twins' first birthday I took them up town to London's Oxford Street, to the John Lewis department store to buy some clothes. I went into the baby changing room to change the girls' nappies; as I took one baby out of the buggy, changed them and put them back in the buggy, then did the same with the second baby, I noticed a few mums just staring at me.

"Oh my gosh, I can't believe you did that so quickly with two kids on your own," one of them said to me.

Another mum said, "I'm actually lost for words. You make it look so easy."

So, we all got talking and I told them the short version of being a new mum of twins and what I had experienced so far as a parent, starting with the health issues I had carrying them, PND, OCD, GAD and sleep deprivation, and the list went on.

One of the mums looked like she was about to cry, one of them hugged me, and another mum said, "And you still found time to comb your hair?" which made me laugh because I knew exactly what she meant.

All I could think at this point was, *these women have no idea what goes on behind closed doors. I really don't have things together at all.*

My intention is not to make motherhood look easy, because my life during the first year was far from the reality they saw, and this wasn't the last time I would hear people telling me I made it look easy. I would get told this all the time—when I took the girls to the park, or to the playground, or a children's party. I don't know what I was doing to make motherhood look so easy.

I suppose when you have a system that works you just get on with it. I didn't think anything of it as it's something I'm just used to doing, but to be honest at that point in my journey of motherhood not many people around me knew what I was going through. I didn't tell a lot of people all the health issues I had or about the PND and OCD. I only started to open up about it when the girls reached around 14 months old.

This was a pivotal point in my life when I started to stop blaming myself for the way I was feeling and the things that were happening to me: the postnatal depression, the anxiety, the stress, the physical pains my body was growing through. I let it all go with the help and support I received from my therapist, my husband and my two best friends in the universe, Ayo and Jazzy. They have been there for me before, during and after pregnancy, and I honestly couldn't imagine life without them. I previously mentioned not being afraid to ask for help if I needed it and these two honestly made it that little bit easier to ask as their presence was always felt even when they weren't there.

So, my advice to you at this stage of parenting would be to appreciate your first year as a parent, reflect on all you've experienced, whether they were positive or negative experiences, and remember you are a survivor and champion of parenthood who has successfully achieved round one.

Always remind yourself that you are doing a fantastic job, be kind to yourself and care for yourself. At this point in your life self-care is vital. Give yourself a break and embrace what you've achieved. Reflecting on the twins' first year, one thing I wish I'd had more time for was self-care. The time for relaxing in a long hot bath with candles, Nora Jones' album playing in the background and no distractions. The time to go the hairdressers and treat myself to a new hairstyle or trim, get a manicure, pedicure and a facial.

Self-care is all about you, involving any kind of action carried out to look after your physical, emotional and mental wellbeing. It's important because it helps to reduce levels of anxiety and improve your mood. It plays a key role in maintaining a healthy and positive relationship with oneself, and provides you with a boost to your self-esteem and confidence. This is exactly what I needed as a new mum because nothing could have prepared me for what I encountered during the first year as a parent.

I have been told plenty of times by mums and dads that the rewards of parenthood are never-ending. Yes, you will have your moments of ups and downs like most parents do, whether you have one child or four children, but the good outweighs the bad and you try your best to be the best parent you can for your children.

My husband and I are in the early stages of parenthood and are looking forward to watching are twins grow, making new memories, exploring, learning and developing. Every day we count our blessings for these two very special gifts that have brought even more joy into our lives.

After our twins turned one and they were confidently walking around I felt so much more at ease. Yes, being able to walk is a challenging new milestone to achieve because that's when children start touching everything and anything they're not supposed to, but I was just glad that I didn't have to keep carrying them because they weren't light in weight, especially when I had one on each hip. Due to me having joint issues in my left hand and right hip, the twins walking was truly a blessing.

When I asked parents how they felt when their multiples turned one I received quite a mixed response. I honestly thought they all felt the same way I did, relieved they were finally one and developing their independence, but this wasn't the case.

"I miss them lying in my arms. All they want to do is run around now they have found their feet."

"They are growing so fast, so quickly."

"Where has the time gone?"

"I miss playing with their tiny little doll's feet."

One thing we all agreed on was how quickly the year went. There I was thinking it was taking a long time when I was in the thick of feeding, changing, bathing, cleaning, but a year went by in a flash.

To keep those first year special memories alive, I have provided you with a table below to list all the precious moments you and your partner experienced with your multiples so that you can reminiscence on them as they get older and eventually show them what you wrote. Whether it's them learning to crawl, taking their first steps or sitting up on their own, jot down as many experiences as you can so you can share it with them when they are older.

Special moments your multiples experienced in the first year

Dates	Times	Places

Surviving the first year of parenting

Kelly Ann from Essex, UK.
Mother of twin girls aged 11.
"When the twins turned one, I was so proud. However, on reflection there's nothing I would have changed apart from the process of weaning the babies of milk onto solids which was awful. They wouldn't eat anything. If I could go back, I would wait longer and try baby-led weaning instead. The best tip I can you give in preparation for surviving the first year would be to have a routine; this will benefit you and your children immensely."

Carmen-Angela from Rostock, Germany.
Mother of triplet girls aged one.
"When my triplets turned one, I was so happy. I couldn't believe that I'd survived the first year and we were happy to celebrate this with our family. I felt like the time had flown by too fast; sometimes I just wanted to turn back time even if there were occasions that were very challenging. Looking back on the first year, my high was that I could breastfeed them until they were one and my low was that I wish I'd done more of holding them in my arms. Although it's a struggle to hold three babies in your arms at once especially when they're crying but it is a regret of mine. Parents with multiples try to have a good sleeping pattern and feeding routine in place in order to survive the first year. This helped us a lot."

Dwayne from London, UK.
Father of twin boys aged eight.

"When my identical twin boys turned one I felt like a proud father who had accomplished something beyond myself. To have not one but two human beings at one time totally reliant on you and actually make it through, healthy and strong, is a massive and great achievement. It was an awesome first year. I can honestly say I wouldn't have changed anything I experienced with my boys in the first year of parenting. Finding your place and space in this new dynamic can be difficult. As a father you feel your duty is to provide and offer support to your partner as and when it's needed. You can sometimes feel lost and forgotten in the process so end up battling with yourself, trying to figure out where you fit in or what you should do and is required of you. That being said, the highs far outweigh the lows, if you focus and feed those highs that is!

Watching two personalities grow and evolve at the same time in their own yet very similar way is just incredible. You learn so much about yourself as a man and father, whilst teaching these two humans how to be a beneficial person to themselves and others in this world.

My best tip to new dads in the same/similar position as me is not to lose yourself; don't compare or get lost in your headspace. There is no comparison! All you have and know is here, now, so live, love and enjoy each and every minute of it! The good, bad and the ugly, ups and downs, negatives and positives. All are valuable and beneficial opportunities to live, learn, grow and evolve as a father!"

Charlotte from London, UK.
Mother of triplets, two girls and one boy aged seven.
"I felt relieved when the triplets turned one, but on reflection

I wouldn't have changed anything on my journey other than tried to have worried less. One of the highlights of the first year was one of my triplets learning how to crawl; this was a special moment. My advice to you for surviving the first year would be try not to worry too much and don't compare your multiples to single children All children are unique."

Cindy from South Africa.
Mother of twin girls aged one.
"I am very proud of myself and my family for surviving the first year of parenthood and how we have raised my twins. To be honest the more they grow the more it gets challenging. I have always wanted them to start walking but now that they are walking, I wish they could go back to being newborns again as they are actively touching everything (I'm smiling to myself as I write this). Looking back, I don't think I would have done anything differently as I'm very happy with the progress they have made. The high of surviving the first year for me was when my twins smiled at me, which put a smile on my face. That overwhelming feeling of seeing them grow milestone to milestone is amazing and the first time they called me mama was so special. The lows for me were the sleepless nights, exhaustion, feeling down at times and them being admitted to hospital for bronchitis. I'm looking forward to seeing how they grow in the future."

Nona from New York, USA.
Mother of triplets, two boys and one girl aged two.
"When my triplets turned one, I was looking forward to their first birthday. One and two years old are my favourite ages.

After the first year, there were fewer feedings and naps which meant more sleep for my husband and I. The babies were sticking to their schedules much better. We had a lot of help and support that I was thankful for. Sometimes it does feel like I miss it a bit, but I think that comes with the territory. Oh, I do wish I'd had a birth photographer to catch all those important pictures to have kept as memories."

The first year with my triplets was quite a gruelling one. I was on a never ending cycle of feeding, napping, soothing, diaper changes, etc. You're in survival mode and only the essentials get done. Showers and brushing your teeth is a treat. The exhaustion is overwhelmingly consuming, but watching them go through their different milestones was fun! The best tip I can give to new parents of multiples is to get help. Get a housekeeper, night nurse, nanny, whatever you can afford. It's a relatively short period of time but oh so intense and getting some sleep makes it much better. Raising multiples can be challenging and tiring so any support you can lay your hands on, take it.

You have now come to the end of my book and I hope you have found it practical, useful and insightful, but mostly helpful. The aim of this book is to support parents like you with useful tips and first-hand experiences of life with multiples, to let you know you are not alone on this new path of parenting multiples. There is help, support and advice available to you through a wide range of services whether its face-to-face, over the phone or online.

No parents will have the exact same experience when raising multiples. Every child is different and has their own personality.

The first year of parenting has its challenges but the rewards outweigh it.

Once you have reached the first year of parenting, multiples life will become a little less complicated, and you will start to feel more like 'you' again. Yes, there will be plenty of new challenges to face as your multiples get older, but it's important you enjoy the moment, take it one day at a time, appreciate what you have and what you've been given. You may have even been able to indulge in some much-needed sleep throughout the night due to having mastered a perfect night-time routine for your multiples, meaning you have more time for yourself and your partner in the evenings which I'm sure you'll appreciate.

As I explained in Chapter 2, being organised in the first year with multiples can be somewhat challenging, something I know I battled with for a while. After having my children I just gave up because I was too tired to try to keep up with all the housework, hospital appointments for La Belle and then of course looking after the girls in general. Now I have more time to organise myself, my family and my household without feeling too stressed or overwhelmed. I have my work-life balance in order. I'm still finding time for some self-care. You'll be able to achieve this too; it may seem like it's far away but it's closer than you think.

Your levels of anxiety might have started to reduce, leaving you feeling less stressed and worried than you were during your pregnancy and in your children's first year. For some of us the feelings of anxiousness may continue as our children age, but it's important we find time to get the support and help we need. Keeping your mental health in check is a priority.

For parents returning to work I am aware that some of you

returned before your children reached their first birthday; some of you may have worked flexible hours or reduced your hours like I did. Returning to work can be seen as both a blessing or a curse depending on your situation, but as I explained in Chapter three and in the tips provided by different parents, it's important you prepare yourself for this transition so that it doesn't take its toll on you.

I was glad to have returned to work as it was a relief for me, but at the same time I felt my maternity leave went very quickly. There were times I wished I could have gone back to work sooner when both girls were screaming at the top of their lungs and there were also times I wished I could have spent longer with my girls because I didn't want to miss any important changes in their development. This might sound contradictory, but that's how I felt some days compared to others and I'm sure there are some parents who felt the same.

I can only imagine there are plenty of parents who never had time for date night thus never considered going out during the first year of having multiples, only thinking about how much sleep they needed and suffering from complete exhaustion. Although this may be the case, all the parents I spoke with agreed that date night was important in a relationship because both parents needed time to unwind, relax, spend quality time together and disassociate themselves from being parents for a few hours. I hope the list of activities I provided for date night can help future parents plan in advance and spend some well-deserved time together alone.

For those of you who have postnatal depression, I hope you find some solace in this book because I know how overwhelming this condition can be. The never-ending mixed emotions you experience can be difficult to cope with, as well as being a parent and having to care for your children at the same time.

As I mentioned, some parents don't even know they have postnatal depression, but what's important is that you ask for help if you're not feeling yourself. In most cases a medical professional will be able to diagnose you and offer you treatment and support.

I know there are some parents who may feel uncomfortable, embarrassed or ashamed to ask for help with their multiples, which should not be the case during such a challenging time in your lives. There is a lot of support available to parents whether it's on or offline but it's important we ask to avoid us feeling as though we are drowning and can't cope.

I also know some parents don't have friends and family close by to support them, however there are organisations parents can turn to for help, support and advice just like the parents I interviewed for this chapter stated in the tips provided. It's very important we ask for help if we need it, as raising one child is hard enough let alone multiples of two, three, four or more.

There I was thinking I was all kinds of crazy for travelling with multiples under the age of one until I realised plenty of parents do it and plenty will in the future. For those of us who have braved the odds and travelled abroad and have had to pack luggage, we know that this can be a daunting task, especially when trying to remember what to pack and how much to pack and whether you are packing the right thing. So, if you are travelling with multiple children under the age of one, the lists I provided are a useful guide of what to pack so please indulge in this. Not everyone packs the same, so you don't need to follow my guide word for word; it's a rough guide as some people have more multiples than others therefore requiring more luggage.

Think about that light at the end of the tunnel. We'll all experience it at some point during the first year of parenting. It can be the smallest thing that your multiples do which makes you smile and helps you see progress is being made. Just remember it's there and life as you know it will get easier as your children get older and learn how to be even more independent.

There will be situations when our children will make us laugh, cry, teach us something new, correct us when we are wrong, but as parents we are here to guide them, tell them how much we love them and how proud we are of them. Our duty is to protect them, keep them safe from harm, nurture them and teach them right from wrong.

In the process of embarking on the next stage of development as parents, we must not forget to include some well-deserved self-care in our lives to ensure we have a positive work-life balance which is essential for our family as whole. Remember that we survived the first year of parenting and will continue to do so for many more years to come.

Lastly, I want to end this book by thanking all the wonderful parents who provided their experiences with their multiples, offering their advice and tips on how to survive the first year of parenting. Thank you for giving up your time to help future parents of multiples on their journey know that they are not alone.

To end, I have provided you with a list of useful websites based on each chapter of this book, which include useful tools, information, advice, help and support throughout your first year as parents. Enjoy the journey and embrace every moment of it. . . as it is true what they say, they really do grow so fast!

Useful websites

CHAPTER ONE – Sleep Deprivation
- https://www.helpguide.org/articles/sleep/sleep-needs-get-the-sleep-you-need.htm
- https://www.mentalhealth.org.uk/blog/importance-sleep
- https://www.nhs.uk/live-well/sleep-and-tiredness/why-lack-of-sleep-is-bad-for-your-health/

CHAPTER TWO – Being Organised
- https://www.nhs.uk/conditions/pregnancy-and-baby/preparing-for-twins-multiples/
- https://www.babycenter.com/609_twins-on-the-way-an-experts-multiple-must haves_20001444.bc
- https://twinsmagazine.com/9-must-have-items-for-twins/
- https://www.thebump.com/a/baby-registry-must-haves-twins-triplets
- https://www.parents.com/baby/twins/caring/your-shopping-checklist-for-multiples/

CHAPTER THREE – Anxiety
- https://www.anxietyuk.org.uk/get-help/anxiety-information/frequently-asked-questions/
- https://adaa.org/about-adaa/press-room/facts-statistics
- https://www.nice.org.uk/guidance/cg192/chapter/Introduction
- https://www.medicalnewstoday.com/articles/323456.php#causes
- https://www.webmd.com/migraines-headaches

- https://www.verywellmind.com/generalized-anxiety-disorder-during-pregnancy-414996
- https://socialphobia.org/social-anxiety-disorder-definition-symptoms-treatment-therapy-medications-insight-prognosis
- https://www.nhs.uk/conditions/social-anxiety/
- https://www.ocduk.org/ocd/introduction-to-ocd
- https://www.tommys.org/pregnancy-information/im-pregnant/mental-wellbeing/specific-mental-health-conditions/obsessive-compulsive-disorder
- https://jamanetwork.com/journals/jamapsychiatry/fullarticle/2652968
- https://www.nhs.uk/conditions/panic-disorder/
- https://www.tommys.org/pregnancy-information/im-pregnant/mental-wellbeing/specific-mental-health-conditions/post-traumatic-stress-disorder
- https://www.verywellmind.com/ptsd-and-physical-health-2797522
- https://www.everydayhealth.com/ptsd/causes-risk-factors-when-seek-help/
- https://www.mind.org.uk
- https://www.postpartum.net
- https://www.anxietyuk.org.uk

CHAPTER FOUR – **Returning to Work**
- https://www.childcare.co.uk
- https://www.citizensadvice.org.uk/work/rights-at-work/parental-rights/maternity-leave-your-options-when-it-ends/
- https://www.gov.uk/maternity-pay-leave

- https://www.nct.org.uk/life-parent/work-and-childcare/returning-work/returning-work-after-maternity-leave
- https://www.acas.org.uk/your-maternity-leave-pay-and-other-rights/returning-to-work-after-having-a-baby
- https://www.moneyadviceservice.org.uk/en/articles/maternity-pay-and-leave

Chapter five – Date Night

- https://www.nhs.uk/live-well/sleep-and-tiredness/why-lack-of-sleep-is-bad-for-your-health/
- https://cpag.org.uk/policy-and-campaigns/report/cost-child-2018
- https://www.mumsnet.com/Talk/parenting/3305759-Anyone-else-s-husband-jealous-of-baby

Chapter six – Postnatal Depression

- https://www.who.int/mental_health/maternal-child/maternal_mental_health/en/
- https://www.nhs.uk/conditions/post-natal-depression/
- https://www.pampers.co.uk/newborn-baby/tips/article/what-are-the-signs-of-postnatal-depression
- https://www.tommys.org/pregnancy-information/im-pregnant/mental-wellbeing/specific-mental-health-conditions/postnatal-depression-pnd

Chapter seven – Don't Be Afraid To Ask

- https://www.babycentre.co.uk/a1047206/get-the-best-out-of-your-health-visitor
- https://www.bliss.org.uk/story/laurens-pnd-story

- https://www.twinstrust.org/let-us-help/pregnancy-and-birth.html
- https://www.twinstrust.org/let-us-help/pregnancy-and-birth/finding-out/triplets-quads-or-more.html
- https://www.nhs.uk/conditions/pregnancy-and-baby/preparing-for-twins-multiples/
- https://www.babycentre.co.uk/a569078/tips-for-raising-multiples
- https://www.kidshealth.org/en/parents/parenting-multiples.html
- https://www.nhs.uk/conditions/pregnancy-and-baby/multiples-postnatal-depression/
- https://www.nct.org.uk/life-parent/how-you-might-be-feeling/postnatal-depression-questions-you-really-want-ask
- https://www.thedadpad.co.uk/
- https://www.dadsmatteruk.org/
- https://www.isablog.co.uk/
- https://www.parents.com/baby/twins/raising/parenting-twins-a-dads-perspective/
- https://www.healthyfamilies.beyondblue.org.au/pregnancy-and-new-parents/dadvice-for-new-dads
- https://www.twinstrust.org/let-us-help/pregnancy-and-birth/finding-out/triplets-quads-or-more.html
- https://www.my1styears.com/blog/life-as-a-triplet-dad/
- https://www.webmd.com/baby/becoming-father-while-remaining-good-partner-twins#1
- https://www.nct.org.uk/life-parent/emotions/postnatal-depression-dads-10-things-you-should-know
- https://www.twinsuk.co.uk/twinstips/28/137/

multiple-males—tips-for-dads-&-grandads-/expectant-father-of-twins-or-more—helping-in-pregnancy/

- https://www.nct.org.uk/pregnancy

CHAPTER EIGHT – Travelling with Multiples

- https://www.sunsense.co.uk
- https://www.childsfarm.com
- https://www.optimah.com (Aloe Pura products)
- https://www.whattoexpect.com/pregnancy/pregnancy-travel-tips
- https://www.nhs.uk/common-health-questions/pregnancy/is-it-safe-to-fly-while-pregnant/
- https://www.babycentre.co.uk/a1019496/how-to-travel-with-twins
- https://www.emmasdiary.co.uk/blog/travelling-with-triplets
- https://www.babycantravel.com/ultimate-guide-travel-with-twins/

CHAPTER NINE – Light at the End of the Tunnel

- www.tommys.org/pregnancy-information/im-pregnant/pregnancy-calendar-your week-week-guide-stages-pregnancy
- https://www.nhs.uk/start4life/pregnancy/
- https://www.babycenter.com/pregnancy-week-by-week
- https://familydoctor.org/condition/de-quervains-tenosynovitis/

About The Author

Leonie Huie is the founder of Empower Me which she started in 2019 after being inspired by her twin daughters to help empower other mothers to improve their work-life balance. After experiencing a challenging pregnancy and giving birth to twins, Leonie suffered from post-natal depression and anxiety, which made it difficult for her to bond with her twins in the first weeks of their life. She returned to work when her babies were 10 months old and struggled to balance work and home life commitments and she knew she wasn't alone. Leonie met so many women with the same issue, trying to manage that elusive work-life balance and still be the best mum they could be whilst providing for their family.

Leonie, who lives in London, now works part-time as a teacher whilst running Empower Me and uses her 17 years' experience in education to coach and deliver training to mothers wanting to make positive changes in their lives to improve work-life balance for themselves and their family. She is also a female empowerment coach, public speaker. Leonie's daughters are still young so she manages her time effectively to ensure she can take them to their favourite place—the park—as well as play games and watch Mr Tumble.